God ∴

SERENITY
GRANTED

ACCEPTING HARDSHIP
AS A PATHWAY TO PEACE

Chris,

Th'll you far?

Richard Preston

your Support
& Inspiration!!

ROSPL

Serenity Granted, LLC

Acknowledgments

If I were to be totally honest, everyone that has ever crossed my path, good or bad, has been an inspiration in writing *Serenity Granted*. I would like to thank my Lord and Savior, Jesus Christ, who died on a rough and rugged cross over 2000 years ago for my sins, transgressions, and atrocities. I am not sure if He takes dedications, so for the rest of us who put our pants on one leg at a time I would like to first thank my wife, Desiree, for putting up with me waking up 4 a.m. each morning to write--I love you. This work could not have been completed without my late parents, James and Mary Preston, all of my brothers, my grandparents, uncles, nieces and nephews, Judge Emmett F. Ferguson III for sentencing me to sanity, my publicist, Sonja Newbill and her husband, my associate pastor, Steve Newbill, the late Laurence Tunsill Jr. (my best friend), and the entire Tunsill family. My pastor and childhood friend, Gary L. Williams, Sr., for his faith in me and helping me to get the first word on paper. Special thanks to Major Richard "Dick" Strommer for his words of wisdom during vulnerable times, my current supervisor, Mr. David Garland, for giving me an opportunity to prove myself. I would like to acknowledge Mr. Lyman "Nap" Johnson for not enabling me in my addiction--I love you, man.

A special thanks to the Banks family on 25th street, Michael Batiste, Timothy "Woody" Monroe, Wilson Holsey, Charles "Fat Cat" Jones and Frank Drummer, my new brothers in Christ, Reverend Timothy Simmons, Pastor Alex Thorpe, Pastor Kevin Smith, Dave Ellison, Deacons Robert Smith and Albert Keaton, my new sisters in Christ, Ms. Weezie, Sharon Woodbine, Olivia Roberts, Linda McInnis, and all the sisters of Hopewell. My circle of friends from high school, Marshall Adkison and his beautiful bride Connie, Jason Burnett and his lovely wife Leslie, Kyle Dean, Benjamin Lundy, Ernest Polite, James McMiller, Doug Lymus, Holly Butler-Sheehan and her extremely funny husband Dan, Mike and Caroline Blue, Al Ferarro and his cute wife Amy, Chap Johnson, Diana Young, Cindy Richotte, Anna Benitez, Ken and Cindy Maroney and their son, Mason. My childhood friend, who is like an extra big brother to me, Roderick Lavender. I would also like to thank The Legend of Largo, Mr. Travis Filer, a true "Funkateer."

I married into a beautiful family so I would like to take the opportunity to acknowledge my beautiful mother-in-law, Jeanette Moses, my sisters-in-law, Charlotte Bennett and Tangie Johnson; my brothers-in-law, Michael Bennett, Demetrius Brooks, and Shane Moses; my stepchildren, Lucretia Becks, Chanel Swindle, and Maurice Glover, my step grandchildren, Chanice Lee, and my step great-grands. Thank you for the extra-special holiday meals to Mrs. Emma Young. I would like to thank all those who believed in me: Ron Green, Rafael and his lovely wife, Skip Thomas, my god brother Simon Moorer, James Lariscy, and my nephew Harold Jackson and his beautiful wife Tiffany and their two children Harold Jr. and Alexis. My sincerest appreciation goes out to my co-workers, Jennifer Macourek, Garry Pope, and Victor Cardenal.

I would also like to acknowledge some of my guests who listened to my testimony-- April Lloyd, Cathy Barnhill, Kathryn and Gentle Groover, Pastor Anthony Willis, Rosilyn Spencer, Kendra Cash, Diana Lencerot, Odella Anderson and Wayne Cotton. A sincere appreciation to my barber, Bryan Jackson and the guys at Lamar's Barbershop on 103rd Street, where every debate is now settled via Google. A very special acknowledgment goes out to anyone suffering from any kind of addiction, it is my prayer that after reading *Serenity Granted*, you will take the first step, which is admitting that there is a problem, and tackling it one day, one hour, and one minute at a time to deliver yourself out of bondage. I want to put in writing what my daughter waited years to hear. Courtney, I cannot replace the time that was not spent together during your formative years (thank God your mother filled that void), events that I missed, talks we never had, tears shed alone, firsts that I never saw but by God's grace and mercy you have grown up to be a beautiful, intelligent, person inside and out, a college graduate and leader in your chosen field of work. I love you and I will be there for you until death. I promise. If by chance I omitted anyone, please forgive me--you know my heart!

Table of Contents

Foreword

Richard Preston, my high school friend, was the typical popular guy. He always did the right things. He was always with the pretty girls and was fun to be around.

I never knew about any addictions that he was dealing with. I honestly don't know what I could have done to help him if I had known. I think how hard it must have been to deal with the addictions.

As years passed, I reconnected with Richard and had the opportunity to meet his beautiful wife, Desiree. Through our old high school friends, we met up after many years and I learned more of what Richard had gone through and how he became clean and sober. Listening to him, I thought, *Wow, what a story!*

Richard lost a part of his life that he could never get back. He lost his family, his friends, and all the money he had earned. I can see how many people would have given up on everything and how people would have given up on him.

The remarkable thing is that Richard never gave up on

himself. He took full responsibility and he worked his way out of his addiction. This story is a true testament to the will-power and strength of a person who wants what most people take for granted. Richard's story will hopefully inspire people who need help conquering their addictions. His story is about hope, hard work, and self-determination. His story also gives perspective to all of us who take every day for granted.

I am honored to know Richard and feel truly blessed to have him in my life! He is not just a friend, but a brother for life. I hope anyone who reads this book will realize the bless-ings they have and the struggles that some people may be dealing with.

Always your friend,

Al Ferraro

Introduction

As I walked across the cream-colored pulpit trimmed in mahogany and accepted the burgundy folder with the diploma that would change my life forever, I wept. It was a certificate of completion that would ultimately signify a regenerated person, a butterfly that had just emerged from the cocoon of an alcohol- and crack-induced coma. A five-cent piece of paper: that was one of the biggest achievements in my life to date. I was a 42-year-old man who really didn't know what it was to be a man. I had all the physical attributes of a person that had been on this planet over four decades--a mustache, a receding hairline, teeth in need of repair. I had no bank account, no driver's license, no stellar resume to present to prospective employers. There was no mortgage to pay, no deadlines to meet, no budget or quota to hit. I read the words over and over: Richard S. Preston has successfully completed all the requirements appertaining to the LEVELS Recovery program and is hereby awarded the rights and privileges of an alumnus. Me. There was more! This recovery program was only a beginning, but it afforded the participant, yours truly, access to the tools necessary to live a wholesome and healthy lifestyle.

On January 31st, 2006, four days after my birthday, I walked into the Salvation Army's Adult Rehabilitation Center in Jacksonville, FL. This was not my first rodeo. but something was different this time. It wasn't the monotonous filling-out of the paperwork that I had become accustomed to, it wasn't the Desk Man that sat behind the oval glass-encased booth as he administered breathalyzers to all beneficiaries entering and exiting the building. It was not the glances that staff members give as they pass by and you intuitively think that they are saying in their mind, "Here comes another loser, again." No, it was nothing about the building, personnel, or déjà vu of the situation. It was me.

I had been on a "Worldwide Reunion Tour" of Rehab Centers--Gateway Rehabilitation Center, River Region Rehabilitation Center, Trinity Rescue Mission; I passed through the Clara White Mission and Sulzbacher Homeless Shelter, The Alumni House and The City Rescue Mission. I would be remiss if I did not mention the institution with the highest rate of recidivism and lowest recovery percentage rate of them all: jail. I was tired, I was broken, I had come to the realization that I was living a life not pleasing to God, my parents, my child, or myself. I was, at the risk of being redundant, sick and tired of being sick and tired.

In 1979 as a ninth-grader at Joseph Stillwell Junior High, I excelled in mathematics, sports, and girls. I was a popular student, I was on the student council, I was the starting small forward on an average basketball team--our colors were red, white and blue and our mascot was the Patriots. I was voted Most Likely to Succeed; little did I know it would be put on hold for twenty-seven years. Today was the first day of the rest of my life. After all, I had just completed a rigorous 30-week course which included over 50 hours of classroom instruction, 120 hours of group therapy, and months of participation in a spiritually based 12-step component, individual and group activities, counseling, work therapy, and transitional and out placement planning. There was the day to day drama of cohabitating with 125 men on a daily basis. Different personalities, backgrounds, and opinions made for some interesting days.

I had an entourage of dignitaries in attendance for my day of reckoning and although humbled by the whole experience, I was as proud as a peacock. My mother held her head high. The judge who had sentenced me was in attendance. Three of my six brothers made it to the ceremony. I had aunts, nephews, cousins, and my godmother and her son were there to share in the accomplishment of the day. The rubber was quickly meeting the road.

I had my tools at hand, my training, and most all, I had faith. An unknown quote states, "God never leads us where He cannot keep us. His grace is always sufficient for us in any and every circumstance of life. When God pushes you to the edge, trust Him fully, because only two things can happen. Either He will catch you when you fall, or He will teach you how to fly." The reason why people give up so fast is because they tend to look at how far they still have to go, instead of how far they have gotten.

CHAPTER 1
The Handwriting on the Wall

I had my first drink at the age of six. It was an instant love affair. My drink of choice, as I remember it, was Old Grandad. It came in a tall, thick glass bottle that was chunky at the base and gently got narrower toward the top. A black top crowned the head of the beast that I did not realize would sooner than later become my best friend and the introduction to my full-blown alcoholism. The label had a beautiful orange hue that resembled the color of navels and mandarins that I had picked while visiting the orange groves in Orlando. It was trimmed in gold and black and it glistened as it sat on my mom's Christmas-decorated dining room table and reflected the light off of her chandelier that was always in need of at least one bulb. A white- haired, smartly dressed Caucasian man was pictured equidistant on the label and had a striking resemblance to one of our founding fathers of this great country. It was as if that bottle was a beacon welcoming me into a world of utter chaos, pain, and deception.

My parents were having an impromptu Christmas celebration for family and friends. The beverages at this affair, as I understood, even at this tender age, were not for me, so I had to devise a plan to reap the benefits of this bounty. Simple. I was well aware that if I just went up to the bottle and poured myself a stiff one, it might not go over very well. After all, I was twelve years south of the legal drinking age in my state. I gazed around the room at knee level and gathered data and inputted it into my microcomputer. A quick analysis of the situation called for immediate action. I gathered my nerves, which at that age, was not hard to do because I was the cute little boy with the dimples, and bowed legs who was walking around in Washington Redskins pajamas with the encased feet so you can walk on the cold of the kitchen floor and still be comfortable. My mom used to call them kitchen pajamas.

The plan was on and popping--should I take the direct approach, or should I try to be as covert as possible? I made my move. I surveyed the different drinks that were pessimistically half empty, and the ones that were optimistically half full. This would be as easy as taking candy from a baby. But there was still a problem--the selections were many. My grandma Ruby was the sole patron, drinking the Old Grandad. She was my maternal grandmother. She was a rotund, jolly woman from Bradenton, FL who now resided in Rochester, NY. She spoke with a hybrid upstate New York and southern accent combined. If you can imagine a mix between Joan Rivers and Paula Deen's voices spliced together, that was my grandmama. She smoked Salem cigarettes at a feverish clip. She ignited her tobacco treats with a monogrammed, gold-plated Zippo lighter that burned using a wick. Opening the lid produced a recognizable "clink" and a different but similar "clunk" when it was closed. She would allow me to blow out the flame if I was in the vicinity when combustion took place. I was fascinated by the smoke and words coming from her mouth and nose in unison like exhaust coming from the tailpipe of a car in winter.

My aunt Emma Joyce was also a part of the Preston's Christmas. She was my mother's sister. Joyce was a school-teacher in Chicago. She was the exact opposite of my mom. She was noticeably younger than my mother and was more hip than square. She never traveled without her collection of fur coats. Why, I would ask myself, would she bring coats that resembled ones that I had seen on explorers during expeditions of the North Pole? She had mink, fox, lynx and chin-chilla. We would always eventually store them at a storage facility on Beaver Street. How ironic.

One year she gave all of us, vests, tams, and scarfs that she had crocheted. Each brother had a different color and they somehow fitted to perfection, as if we were measured from head to toe for the overspun yarn masterpieces. We would put on the outfits and call ourselves The Preston Seven, singing and playing air guitars trying to emulate the hottest band at the time, The Jackson Five. Emma Joyce was drinking Cutty Sark, a blended scotch whisky. It came in in a lizard-green-colored bottle and stood out noticeably from the other luscious libations. The label on the bottle was stoplight yellow and had a picture of either the Niña, Pinta or Santa Maria proudly displayed under the name of the product. The picture was illustrated in such a way that the ship seemed to be gently tossing in the waves.

My cousin Buster, aka Doc, was a staple at our home for more than just holidays and special occasions. He was my daddy's most-beloved relative. I never heard my father--or anybody else, for that matter--utter a bad word about Doc. Whenever he came over to visit, one of us kids would have to surrender the most comfortable chair to Doc. My mom would scramble to assemble some sort of impromptu hors d'oeuvre to serve, usually a summer sausage sliced on a Ritz cracker or my father's famous homemade hogshead cheese on a saltine if he was lucky. Buster was drinking a clear beverage and seemed to be mixing it with orange juice. When my mother asked him if he would like another screwdriver, I was puzzled. At this age, I could not associate a hand tool that is used to adjust the brakes on my Western Flyer, with a drink of my choice.

There were other choices for my first happy hour as well. Cans of beer were left unattended on the coffee table. Budweiser, Miller High Life, and Pabst Blue Ribbon were the suds of choice this evening. I began a process of elimination. The glasses that had cigarette butts in them were out of the question; next on the list were glasses with lipstick on them, I hated lipstick. It was always on my mother's friend's lips who found me to be adorable enough to squarely kiss me on my mouth as I shopped with her in the grocery buggy at the neighborhood Daylight grocery store. They, the adults, were making it easy for me and I was getting an education on how to be cunning all at the same time. The music was playing from our state of the art Magnavox console stereo. It was a radio, 8-track tape player, record player and television bundled together as one in a beautiful walnut veneer cabinet.

Huge 13-inch woofers were built in on both ends of the monstrosity and small tweeters were conspicuously hidden in the web of wires and vacuum tubes. The Temptations were on "Cloud Nine" and Gladys Knight and her Pips were taking the "Midnight Train to Georgia." Each time the song got to the part where the Pips did their infamous onomatopoeia, Woo! Woo! as the train scurried on back to the Peachtree State, everyone in the room would shout it out in unison. They were having a good time and I was about to have mine.

As a raptor locks in on his prey, I decided on a golden-colored partially consumed drink that still had ice cubes that resembled glaciers floating in an Alaskan bay. I made my final approach from the hallway, the kitchen pajamas came in handy as there was no carpet in our hallway, I briefly paused at our telephone table circa 1950. The family's one tan rotary dial phone was a fixture on the old, rickety, but well-kept table. I was careful not to trip over the seemingly fifty feet of cord that was tangled and knotty. We had only one phone in the house for all eight people and that line stretched from my parents' room to the back porch. I stepped over it like a thief in the night. I made my way over to the demon that would inevitably become my nemesis for decades. I picked up the drink and carried it away as if I was a sailor at a bar in some foreign land after months on the open sea. The smell of the alcohol permeated my nostrils. The aroma of the aged spirits was orgasmic. I didn't even have to taste it to know that I was in love. It was a match made from heaven and hell at the same time. We made our vows and I exclaimed in my mind. I do. It was time to consecrate the union of boy and substance.

The magical elixir poured over my tongue and down my

narrow throat. It trickled ever so slowly over my virgin taste buds. I sighed. I never flinched, although this new drink was more powerful than any grape, strawberry, or cherry Kool-Aid I had ever tasted. It was much better, in a peculiar way. I had found my Bonnie and I was Clyde. It opened my eyes in a way they had never been opened. The euphoria that was happening was like waking up on Christmas morning and seeing Santa had made his rounds and helped himself to most of the pound cake that Mom had made exclusively for him.

I took another sip and worked the room. Before I could finish the first drink, I was already preparing for my second round. My newfound friend was giving me courage. The music was sounding better. The lights shined brighter from that old chandelier. The voices in that small living room became a cacophony of sounds echoing from wall to wall. I had entered into a state of mind that was relaxing and calm. I feared no evil. I finished the first drink of my life. It was one too many and one shy of not enough. Superman had met his kryptonite. But unlike Clark Kent, who knew what would reduce his superhuman powers to nothing...I did not.

I repeated the act over and over again, just as an offensive coordinator of a football team uses a successful play until his opponent stops it. I was oblivious to what was transpiring. I knew what I was doing was wrong and there would be grave consequences to pay if I was caught, but the pleasure, excitement, and feeling of being inebriated for the first time in my life overshadowed the threat of being apprehended by any of the adults. I felt invincible at this juncture; I came to the conclusion in my young, twisted mind that I was the smartest person in the room. This was not new to me. I was the most intelligent kid in my kindergarten class. I could read better than anyone in the group. I could use construction paper, paste, and scissors more efficiently than my counterparts. I could make a snake, a ball, and even a house out of clay better than any of my peers. I excelled in everything that had been put before me so far in life and alcohol was shaping up to be no different.

I awoke--or came to--the next morning to jeers and laughter from my brothers as my mom rushed into my room. It was like a scene from an old movie when the person suddenly awakens from a coma. She was wearing her old tattered pink terry cloth bathrobe, and old blue slippers that had seen their better days but were the most comfortable shoes that she owned. Mom had a look on her face that I had never seen before. It was a face of sadness, like that of a basketball player who had missed an easy layup that could have won the championship game. Like a father who knows for sure that his little girl is no longer a virgin. She held me tight to her bosom and looked deep into my eyes and asked me how was I feeling? I could feel her heart beating in rhythm. It was steady but not fast. I could sense that I had somehow let her down. It was a feeling that only mother and child can describe.

I tried to speak, but no words came out of my mouth. She delicately put her index finger over my lips and whispered in an angel's voice, "It's going to be okay, baby!" She rocked me and prayed an inaudible prayer that seemed to go on for eternity. After ending the prayer with a heartfelt "God bless you and amen," she placed me back into the bed and tucked me in with the skill and precision of a surgeon.

My brother Charles came in the room and stared at me

as I tried to figure out why my mama was in extra overdrive, attention, and love mode on this particular Saturday morning. Charles was my partner in crime. He was three years my senior and very intelligent. He was tall and thin and could run like a deer. Like gold is the standard on which our monetary system in America is measured against, my brother Dap (as he would affectionately become known as nicknamed, from the character Dap Sugar Willie who did cameo appearances in successful black sitcoms in the '70s) set the bar for me at a very high standard. He was the person I wanted to be. He saved his coins, his pencils were always razor-sharp and without burs, his erasers seemed to never have had to make any corrections--they were always clean and had sharp angles. I marveled at him and was amazed how he would always eat his vegetables first and save his entrée to savor and enjoy at the end of every meal, ensuring that his last recollection of a meal would be chicken, beef, pork, or seafood and not beets, turnips or green beans.

Dap came up to the side of the bed and asked me in confidence as he looked at the door that he closed behind him as he entered the room and asked, "Do you remember what you did last night?"

More startling than the question that he had just put before me was the answer. "No, I don't," I said as I was grappling with the situation.

"Joyce found you asleep in the bathtub this morning."

Could he be serious? My brother was not only smart, but he was known to pull a fast one on you, too. But as much as I wanted this to be a hoax, the expression on his face was indicating that it was not. His body language and demeanor were those of sympathy and fear. He knew that at any instant, the door of that tiny aqua-green-colored room was going to fling open and anyone caught sympathizing with the prisoner might have to answer to the same charges as said defendant. We understood that the promises of "wait until I tell your father about this" rarely occurred; we had become to know this to be a warning or threat, but only actually carried out in the severest of cases. This was a scare tactic with a 100 percent success rate, because the level of the infraction was always subjective and in direct proportion to what was going on at the moment, how my Father's Day was going, and ultimately how it was going to affect the peace or lack thereof in the house on that given instance.

I nervously listened for my father's footsteps to head in my direction; the agony of not knowing if my mom had informed the warden was torturous. I didn't want to get up, I didn't want to answer any questions, I didn't want to go outside and play with any of my friends. I had come full circle in less than 24 hours. I had my first drink, got drunk, experienced my first blackout, and now the guilt and shame was eating at the core of my very existence. I am an alcoholic.

CHAPTER 2
The Pursuit of Pleasure

I was treated more like a victim than the perpetrator for the first-degree felony committed Christmas Eve 1970. I was given a lecture on the dangers of drinking, but since I was never punished corporally, I knew what I had done could not have been all that bad, because the breaking of a vase, lying, or not doing my homework brought on much stiffer consequences--up to and including a blistering of the behind. The news spread like wildfire in California during a drought and circulated the neighborhood faster than any tweet or post on Twitter or Facebook could ever imagine. The events of the evening had been leaked to neighbors and relatives, so I was subjected to the teasing and taunting from my friends as we played basketball down in the 1900 block of 24th Street in front of the field, where we had a hoop made of materials that we found or nabbed from various spots. The rim, which was obviously the most important part of the structure, had been ripped off its perch from the courts located behind Susie E. Tolbert Elementary School across the 20th Street Expressway (later to be named MLK Expressway, after the assassinated civil rights leader), which was a major divide in our neighborhood. My brother, friends, and I had to cross this four-lane Autobahn each morning to get to school. The highway was also used as a social dividing line in our neighborhood. The families on the north side of the MLK Expressway appeared to be more hot dogs, apple pie, and Chevrolet. The two-parent household was the norm than the exception. Ironically, I was always trying to get to the other side.

My father, James R. Preston, Sr., was born February 29, a leap year, to Mr. Joseph Lee Preston and Mrs. Dora Preston, née Dennis, in Baldwin, Florida in 1916. He was a tall man with salt-and-pepper hair and was proud of his boys. My dad was a World War II veteran and retired from the United States Post Office after thirty-seven years of dedicated service. He was stern but fair. His primary goal in life was to take care of his family and raise strong, polite, educated men. Although he was raised in the height of oppression and segregation, he did not have a prejudiced bone in his body. He did understand however, the differences between black and white, often telling horrifying stories of how he was treated as a boy and even as a sailor who was drafted to serve his country in the biggest War in our country's history, but he never let that interfere with his mission for his children. Using the color of our skin as a crutch or justification for poor performance in life was not an option. I never once experienced him playing the proverbial race card. He truly believed that every man was created equal and that we are endowed by our Creator with certain inalienable rights, as stated in the Declaration of Independence of the United States of America.

We affectionately called our paternal grandmother "Mama Dora." She was a short, silver-haired, very quiet lady who lived all alone in a small white house in the country. She was born Dora Catherine Dennis on December 8, 1899 in Margaretta, Florida. She received her early education in the public schools of Baker County, which is west of Duval County. She was always smartly dressed and her silky curly hair was always curled and tight, all without aid from a weave or hair extensions. She wore colorful floral dresses that fit her small-framed body like a glove. She would accentuate the outfit with a small cardigan sweater, not with her arms through the sleeves, but elegantly placed over her shoulders that exuded grace and sophistication. It was always my dream to have her live until the year 2000 so she could say that she lived in three different centuries. She lived to be ninety-four and died in 1994. Her house was centered between US 90 on the south and US 301 on the north in Baldwin, Florida. It was located on an unpaved road that had a ditch in front of the house, sandwiched between woods in the front and back yard. The house was marked by a chain-link fence that surrounded its perimeter. A small, neatly kept garden that seemed to always have a different bounty growing in its rows was just yards from the rear entrance to the property. The back of her fairy-tale-looking cottage faced the street and the front faced the woods--a juxtaposition that I would not figure out until I was an adult.

After church each Sunday, my parents and all my brothers would pack into our 1964 Chevrolet Impala station wagon and head to Baldwin. The white behemoth had more than enough interior room to hold us safely and comfortably. It had a blood-red interior, bench seats in the front and rear, and a powerful V8 engine under the hood. The car had enough storage space for us to bring the essentials for a great family outing. Football, basketball, baseball bats and gloves, and a homemade cake prepared by my mom's loving hands to present to her beloved mother in law as a loving expression for having us over and putting up with all of the little darlings were always neatly packed in the car. The last item to be stored in the car was my father's adult beverage of choice. This was usually wrapped in a brown bag or in its original decorated box. After surviving the Christmas party debacle, I was now fixated on the whereabouts of the alcohol and planning a strategy to have drinks at my disposal.

Paradoxically, being a city boy I hated going out to the country, but I knew the trip generally offered the easiest opportunity for me to sneak a drink or two. While my brothers were unknowingly diverting attention away from me as they threw rocks at wild rabbits, picked berries for one of my mother's famous blackberry doobies (a pie with no bottom crust) or trying to retrieve water from the old rusted hand-cranked pump located in the middle of my grandmother's yard that we were warned each visit not to touch. The rationale for not touching everything was that we might hurt ourselves, which translated into we might hurt whatever we were touching.

I usually planned my escapades to coincide with after-dinner banter and laughter. Miss Dora, as the natives called my grandmother, made a fried chicken that would run Popeye's back to Olive Oyl, Church's would lose their religion, and the Colonel would be demoted back to Private. So after the last piece of chicken was taken from the deep dish that was lined with a red- and-white plaid towel that she used instead of paper towels to absorb the excess cooking oil, it was cocktail hour. This was no different than what I was seeing on the television screen--it was simply a social time. This was what I saw on almost every TV show that I watched.

My favorite show at the time was *Bewitched*, an American sitcom that ran from 1964 to 1972. It starred Elizabeth Montgomery as Samantha and Dick York (1964-1969) and Dick Sargent (1969-1972) as her husband Darrin. It was here that I noticed that drinking was part of the social fiber of their existence, just as it was in my home. The settings were different but the overall objective seemed to be the same. Drinking was for beautiful people, sexy people, and the one that really sank in was that it seemed to be linked to successful people as well. The bigger the occasion, the more they drank, and no occasion was bigger for me than a Sunday in Baldwin.

The time spent in this rural western corner of our county is where I gradually started perfecting the craft of getting tipsy. I was getting bolder in my attempts to satisfy what was quickly becoming a need to attain the pleasure that I associated with consuming alcohol. As the years passed and I approached double digits in age, I was brazen enough to just open the refrigerator and help myself to the liquid devil that seemed so right at the time. I also noticed that I got a rush not only from the substance itself but from the pursuit of procuring my new-found friend. Lying, which is a common trait of alcoholics, was becoming very easy to do where it had not been before. The thrill of the chase was just as intense as the kill itself. The planning, plotting, and process were equal to the mood-altering effects of the liquid gold.

CHAPTER 3
Progressively Paralyzed

In my adolescent years, I was developing into a nice young man on the exterior. Integration was introduced into our city in 1973 and I was bused to the Arlington area of town and attended Merrill Road Elementary #228. It was a newly built, yellow brick, air-conditioned school east of the St. Johns River nestled among shady oaks, and huge homes with manicured lawns and swimming pools. The campus had a huge playground and was surrounded by densely thick woods. My new school stressed parent involvement and my mother was all in--anything to help her baby succeed. There were paper drives, a contest to see who could bring in the most recyclable paper products, PTA meetings, and parent-teacher conferences. We lived about fifteen miles away from the school and had to cross the John E. Mathews Bridge, a cantilever bridge named after a Florida state legislator and Chief Justice of the 1955 Florida Supreme court. The span connected downtown to the suburbs of Jacksonville.

My teacher, Mrs. Pickard loved me. I can only imagine

why but if I had to guess, it was because I was crushing every stereotype that she had in her mind about blacks, just as the white kids were dispelling all the preconceived notions about them to me. Nobody in that classroom was perfect. I was on the A-B honor roll each nine-week period. I had the highest score on the Collegiate Fundamental test. I proudly won the Spelling Bee that year. Mary and James were raising the ideal kid, or so they believed. I was well-behaved and I excelled in the world of academia. I maintained a 4.0 grade point average or better by taking advanced courses that offered an extra point in the grading system. I was well-spoken, confident and did quite well with the girls if I do say so myself.

Back in the neighborhood, I attended Henry Gordon African Methodist Episcopal Church, a small white church with a modest steeple that seemed to be always in need of a paint job. It was located on the corner of 25th Street and Wilson Street. My brothers and I made up about a quarter of the congregation at the small church. We were vital cogs in the services each Sunday. I was the secretary, my older brothers were Sunday school teachers, and we all doubled as ushers. After church, the monies that were not put in the old tin collection plates that had little round circles of red carpeting placed in the middle to muffle the sound of coins being dropped into them was spent at the corner confectionery store. This quaint, purple-colored building was a treasure chest for purchasing the most popular candies. The treats ranged from all flavors of Now and Laters, soft chews, and Twisters, a hard flavorful candy that is the ancestor of what we call a Jolly Rancher today. My favorite was a candy made by the Ferrara Pan Candy Company called Lemonheads. They were a lemon-flavored candy consisting of a sweet coating, soft sour shell and a hard candy core. They came in a small rectangular box that instantly became a homemade harmonica after all the sugary pieces were devoured.

We would finish our visit at the store by playing and trying to master the pinball machine. The pinball machine is an American iconic arcade game, usually coin-operated (a nickel back in those days) in which points are scored by manipulating a steel ball on a play field inside a glass-covered cabinet.

We would arrive home from church to a house that smelled of a Sunday dinner. My father was not very fond of chicken so it was usually a roast, smothered steak, or a ham. The vegetables (they weren't called "sides" in those days) were usually collard, mustard, or the notoriously funky turnip greens. The one constant would be that they were fresh, either hand-picked from my grandmother's garden or purchased the day before from the farmers' market on West Beaver Street. The delicacies were usually stripped and cleaned the night before as the family watched *Mutual of Omaha's Wild Kingdom* co-hosted by Marlin Perkins and Jim Fowler. This show can be credited for increasing ecological and environmental awareness in the United States. Its exciting footage brought the wilds of Africa, the Amazon River, and other exotic locales into the living rooms of millions of Americans each week, and ours was no different. We also watched *Hee Haw*, a country comedy and variety show hosted by Roy Clark and Buck Owens. The show was equally known for its voluptuous, scantily-clad women in stereotypical farmer's daughter outfits and country-style mini dresses.

After the night's entertainment was over and all chores

were done, my mother would retire to her bedroom, her inner sanctum from the rest of the world, a place where she would sit in front of her mirror combing her beautiful locks-- and as I look back, thank God for her many blessings, and she had many. She was born January 15th, 1927 in Bradenton, Florida, a small town just south of Tampa in Manatee county. She played tennis and basketball. She and my father, a WWII veteran, were married on May 10, 1947. Her smile would light up a room and her voice was soft and sweet. She once sang "Oh Come All Ye Faithful" into a small Realistic Cassette tape recorder that I had gotten for Christmas one year and it was the sweetest rendition of that Christmas song that I ever heard. This is without question my favorite Christmas carol of all time. She was gentle as a lamb, but she could be stern when she had to be--and she had to be often, with seven boys. She was the love of my life. I would spend the next thirty-five years looking for that perfect woman to marry, my mother.

While my mom was preparing the supper, my dad was usually sitting in the living room reading the newspaper in his favorite chair and drinking a beer. I had devised two ways of getting my drink on the Sabbath. The first was to be a nice son and offer to take his old beer away and get him an ice-cold one out of the fridge. Using this method, I would drink the last of the old beer and drink the top off of the new beer because I would really go the extra mile and open it for him. In the pre-recycling era, the tabs were literally pulled off the cans and discarded. I would even lick the excess off the curled-up sharp-as-a-razor tab to taste the refreshing brew. My second method was more primitive and simple. I would simply wait for nature to call and when my dad would excuse himself to the lavatory, I would take one big huge gulp or a couple of small sips. I noticed that beer was starting to taste just as good as the buzz that I was experiencing from drinking the fermented collection of hops, barley, and malt. I could swallow larger quantities at a time, I wasn't grimacing as much when I did ingest the fruits of my deception, and the smell of my liquid libations was becoming more aromatic to me than a bouquet of flowers swaying in a cool summer breeze.

In junior high school came more freedom and trust, and with those liberties in place my drinking increased. In 1977 I was attending James Weldon Johnson 7th Grade Center. Born in Jacksonville in 1871, Mr. Johnson was a great American author, politician, diplomat, critic, journalist, poet, anthologist, educator, lawyer, songwriter, and early civil rights activist. His accomplishments are many but he is best known for his song "Lift Ev'ry Voice and Sing," now considered to be the "Black National Anthem." My chest hairs had emerged, my voice was getting deeper--and so was my interest in the darker side. I was the point-forward on the basketball team. We did not lose a game that year or even come close to losing one thanks to our MVP Todd. Todd was a Caucasian athlete who dispelled the myth that "white guys can't jump." He could jump, shoot, run, and score better than anyone on the team. We were crowned champions of the city that year, and I was named Defensive Player of the Year.

James Weldon Johnson happened to be located on the south side of the 20th Street Expressway. This was the side that had most of the off-limits places for us, as declared by my father. My next-door neighbor and one of my mom's closest friends, Mrs. Emily Nicholson, was a teacher at our school. Miss Emily, as I still call her to this very day, was an art instructor at JWJ. She was a thin, pretty pecan-skin-colored lady who spoke in a quiet, measured voice. Where my mom was a housewife and her morning attire was a bathrobe and slippers, Miss Emily dressed professionally and her outfits were smart, crisp, sharp, and screamed of success. I would ride to school with her each morning, but because a teacher's day was longer than mine, I would walk the fourteen blocks home each day.

I had learned from other drinking buddies that I could actually buy the goods for myself. The place was E and Y Diner, located at the corner of Myrtle Avenue and west 15th Street. I rode my 10-speed Black Western flyer bicycle with dual mirrors and an aftermarket speedometer that I had added from money earned doing odd jobs in the neighborhood to the happening spot. I arrived at my destination. I chained my bike to the newspaper machine with the words *Jacksonville Journal* printed on one side and a view of the daily gazettes on the other. The building was a half-brick, half-glass structure that was adjacent to Dr. Arnett Girardeau's dentist's office; he would later become a Florida State Senator.

I approached the door that had the business hours handwritten on a decal that was glued to the thick, dark-tinted glass. The place was dark and reeked of smoke, fried chicken, and cheap wine. I looked around and let my eyes adjust to the dimly lit café. The jukebox was playing Johnny Taylor's "Who's Making Love" and a tall dark-skinned lady with hoop earrings and a dashiki (a west African loose-fitting pullover garment with an ornate V-shaped collar) was standing in front of the loud, glass-enclosed music machine with dollar bills cupped in her hand, singing each lyric as she and her well-trimmed Afro swayed to the beat.

I approached the counter with reluctance and trepidation. As I began to speak, a drunken patron butted in front of me to ask for a light. That gave me a few more seconds to calm down and make sure that my words came out in a low tone of voice like Barry White, the smooth baritone crooner known for making the ladies melt, and not Norville "Shaggy" Rogers the cowardly slacker from the animated series Scooby-Doo. At age thirteen it was like a crap shoot each time you opened your mouth to speak so deep was good. I asked the clerk with assurance and certainty for a bottle of Champale. This adult beverage was a brand of malt liquor, brewed with yeasts more commonly used in wine fermentation, to produce a beer resembling sparkling wines in taste. It was one of the first alcoholic drinks to target the African-American market in its advertising. The drink was pitched as a "poor man's champagne" with slogans such as "Live a little on very little."

She asked me, "Sparkling or pink?"

Shaggy almost reared his ugly head, but after a quick clearing of the throat, Barry belted out, "Sparkling!" She went over to the condensation-covered cooler, reached in the back and intuitively organized her inventory, and slipped my bounty into a brown paper bag that exposed the neck of the bottle where the name was embossed. I looked around as if I were passing a "stick-up note" to a bank teller during a bank robbery. I fumbled for my wadded-up one-dollar bills that I had tucked in my Levi corduroy jeans. I moved slowly in dreaded anticipation for the two words that I was waiting to be asked: *Identification, please.*

"That will be $1.75 please, sir."

She called me sir. I gave her the folded, sweaty money and told her to keep the change. She smiled and wished me a happy day. It was a victory of a battle in a war I was destined to lose.

I did an about-face and was redirected to the west side of town for my 8th and 9th grade school years. Joseph Stilwell was located off I-10 west about twelve miles from my Northside home in a rural section of town called Marietta. The school sat off the road and was almost hidden by scores of oak trees with what looked like centuries of overgrown moss hanging from the gargantuan branches. The ground was littered with leaves, twigs, and acorns. The building was constructed of yellow brick and the roof had a steep slope that was braced by a row of huge steel columns that supported both sides of the structure. The super-sized supports were painted blue and red, our school colors. I was now a Patriot. I could not wait to see the gym, since I had already made a name for myself on the hard court by starting on a city championship team that didn't lose a single game. Seasons like those are hard to come by on any level. The incumbent players on the varsity squad had made it their business to seek me out and introduce themselves because they knew that I would have one of their positions because the junior varsity team was not an option for me. The gymnasium would not disappoint; it had a beautiful newly finished hardwood court that shone like Madison Square Garden.

It was here that I met my best friend for life, Mr. Laurence

Isaiah Tunsill, Jr. Laurence was an athlete with skills that gained him star status. He was always the leading rusher back in our YMCA peewee football days, the leading scorer on the basketball team and for fun he was the star of the softball team. He was a lighter-skinned guy with a thick, soft, Michael Jackson-style Afro. He had doe-like big, brown, sparkling eyes that were charming and sincere. The character that his eyes possessed went far beyond the pigment and hue; they reflected emotion, intelligence, and life. He was built like O.J. Simpson and ran like a gazelle. We had never been formally introduced because I was too busy being trampled by him trying to tackle him when my Susie E. Tolbert team was trying our best to match up with his Mary McCloud Bethune squad as we battled for supremacy on the small field of the Young Man's Christian Association (YMCA) located on Cleveland road. He was not only a gridiron and hardwood champion. He was an urban legend. Like all legends, "Little Laurence," as his mother called him, had a mysterious personality. He was funny yet serious, he was cautious yet kind, he embellished all his accolades with humility and used them in a way to help others perform to the best of their God-given ability.

I went on to start as a forward for the varsity team that year. Laurence didn't start, but he never held it against me-yet I did feel some animosity from some of the other guys who had to "ride the pine," or whose playing time was greatly reduced because I was having a break-out season. The previous year I was counted on to stop the other team's top scorer, but I was now depended on to score for this team and I did not disappoint, averaging 15 points per game. We prepared for the biggest game of the year with our rivals the Lake Shore

Warriors with intense practice sessions. This was an in-school game and all of the students, teachers, and parents would be in attendance. This is the game of the year, the game where you go from having forty fans to a packed house. All of the retractable bleachers that were made of a hardwood marred by the engravings of teenagers from years past would be used to house the standing-room-only crowd. Everybody who never saw us play would now get the chance to see us in action. The principal, dean of students, teachers, janitors, cafeteria staff, and classmates were all in attendance to cheer us to victory. Fortunately, we won the game and I had a game high-22 points. Laurence and I celebrated after we got home by riding our bikes up to my new found favorite establishment and purchased four quarts of Champale to celebrate the victory.

Tracy introduced Laurence and me to marijuana. He was well dressed, came to school with an attaché case, wore jewelry and cologne and his last name differed from his father's surname. He lived across the street from Laurence with his grandmother on 30th Street in a small yellow brick house. Tracy never mentioned his mother, which I thought was odd, but I never questioned him about his lineage. He had a moustache and goatee; his demeanor and the way he conducted himself was years ahead of me and my friend. His wardrobe was even different from what was considered hip for a four-teen-year-old. He sported the latest styles from men's clothiers like the Funk Trunk, Movin' Man, and Jack Mr. Highstyles--a sharp contrast to my J.C. Penny, Montgomery Wards and for the rare occasions when May Cohen had a merchandise clearance apparel sale.

I liked the smell and the effects of the weed that was so

freely provided to me and eventually was smoking it every day as we waited at the bus stop. We also had a connection to purchase beer from a neighborhood store that was literally a block from my house. This store was run by an old man and his wife from their home. They had erected a small unassuming addition to the side of the dwelling that was used to sell confections, snacks, soda and his famous Bon Ton brand of potato chips. The proprietor of this handy emporium was a tall, thin man who seemed to be not in the greatest of health. His cheekbones were sucked in and his mouth was always moving as if he were chewing food. We nicknamed him "The Praying Mantis." He didn't speak much, was never in a good mood, and wore a "wife beater" T-shirt with dark- colored slacks which seemed to be the same ones every day, and chain smoked Winstons. He also sold, without any questions asked, what had quickly become my favorite beverage: beer. The breakfast for these champions was not Wheaties, Apple Jacks, or Cocoa Puffs but the most important meal of the day was a Schlitz Malt Liquor, Old English 800 Malt Liquor, Colt 45 Malt Liquor, and pot.

According to Rhonda Webb-Jones, associate professor in the School of Public Health at the University of Minnesota, malt liquors are largely targeted to African-American and Hispanic youth and young adults. "They are used by the alcohol industry to connote power and machismo and lure them into the market." Ricky Bluthenthal, assistant professor at Charles R. Drew University of Medicine and Science states, "Because of the container size and alcohol by volume, some as high as 12 percent, malt liquor drinkers in his study consumed 80 percent more alcohol per drink than average regular beer drinkers. Typically, the more alcohol consumed, the greater the probability of negative alcohol-related consequences for an individual and their community." I was an ethnographic study playing out in real life, real time, and with real consequences. The need to have my mind altered by foreign substances was becoming increasingly apparent. There were some days when we couldn't scrounge up enough money for both the marijuana and beer, but in those rare cases when we did not, beer was only lunch money away and my parents supplied me with that every day.

The next time we played our rivals, Lakeshore, it was at their gym and it was a teachers' planning day so there was no school, and the game plan was to meet at the visitors' gym one hour before game time. I hooked up with Laurence at his house that morning. I was finding a new freedom at that small brown house on 30th Street. The house that he shared with his brothers Errol, Lance, and Lyle was about twenty years newer than our house and had all the modern conveniences, including a gas stove, carport, and a utility room. Instead of the common white walls that I was familiar with, this house had an earthy look. The walls were decorated in earth tones and wood paneling. It was dimly lit and smelled of fresh herbs and fruit.

His parents were thirty years (or so it seemed) younger than my parents and vastly different in ideals, nutrition, and beliefs. They were a progressive family. I affectionately called his dad Mr. T, short for Tunsill, their last name--and his mom was simply Miss Nellie. Mr. T was a short man full of laughter and wisdom. Miss Nellie was a sleek, slender, soft-spoken woman with elegance, grace, and charm. She wore her hair in a neatly well-trimmed Afro with no strand ever out of place. She reminded me of an African goddess. No makeup, no excessive jewelry--just plain beauty inside and out. His parents were longtime employees of the phone company. My dad had retired from the post office and my mom was always a housewife, so for both parents to be gone from the home for eight hours and having total freedom, so to speak, was as foreign to me as living on the moon. During those hours we came and went as we pleased, ate and cooked what we wanted, listened to music as loud as we wanted, and drank as much as we wanted. This was Shangri-La.

I had my first sexual encounter at this house. I had kissed girls and rubbed on girls for hours until it hurt. But this one was for real. Her name was Jackie; we had gone to school together since elementary. She was tall, thin, and very funny. She lived on the "other" side of the expressway behind the neighborhood Burger King. It was as hard for her to escape her parental guidance as it was for me, but we made it happen. I picked her up on my Western Flyer and rode her on the handlebars over to 1947 W. 30th Street and both of us lost our virginity. Laurence and I hung out that morning of the big game and purchased a 7-cent bag of weed. The number value associated with the illegal goods denoted how much it cost and the quantity of the smoke. We jumped the ditch and found an abandoned railroad car and rolled 15 small joints for the day's festivities. We smoked and drank like it was New Year's Eve in New York. We eventually made it to the basketball game on time and joined our team for warm-ups. I noticed that I was lethargic and sluggish during layup drills. My motivation and confidence were lacking as well. All eyes from the opposing team were on me since I had torched them the last time we played--but tonight was not going to be my night; I could sense it.

From the moment the ball was tipped off until the final buzzer, I was a non-factor. I was called for more fouls than points scored, I missed important defensive assignments, I even missed a snowbird--that is an open route to the basket with nobody within 20 feet of you. The coach had no idea what was going on, but Laurence and I had our suspicions. We lost that game but the game of life was still going on and I was a starting player...or so I thought. I attributed my lackluster performance to just having a bad night, but I was playing with fire and destined to be burned. If hindsight is 20/20--and it is--the statistic that I should have been fully aware of was by 8th grade, 52% of all adolescents have consumed alcohol, 41% have smoked tobacco, and 20% have used marijuana. Compared to females, males are four times as likely to be heavy drinkers, according to The Treatment Center.com. The study goes on to say that social learning is considered the most important single factor in addiction. It includes patterns of use in the addict's family or subculture, peer pressure, and advertising or media influence.

Peer pressure was a contributing factor with a large percentage of bad choices that I was making, but advertising was subconsciously pulling me into the vortex of the tornado disguised as a good time. The Joseph A. Schlitz company had it going on with malt liquor commercials boasting that if you wanted to be hip, have beautiful women surrounding you, and be dashing and debonair, then this was the must-have product. "Nobody does it like the bull," "Put the bull where your beer is," "Don't say beer, say bull," were exclaimed by some of the most popular black entertainers of that generation. Richard Roundtree, the star of arguably the biggest black exploitation movie of the '70s, Shaft, walks into a bar on one of the commercials that still conjures up an image in my head forty years later where he strides into the smoke-filled bar loaded with beautiful chicks playing the theme song from that iconic movie, and as he enters the place the music lowers and he inquires, "What's going on besides beer?"

Antonio Fargas, who played Huggy Bear, the paid confidential informant on the hit TV series Starsky and Hutch, replies, "Bull."

The music stops and Roundtree retorts that he will turn this place into a car wash. Fargas explains, "No, the Schlitz Malt Liquor Bull--it has more taste than beer." The music pumps back up and Roundtree grabs one and a woman, and the party continues. The commercials featured notables such as Teddy Pendergrass, the deep-voiced R&B singer that all the ladies adored, and The Four Tops, an American vocal quartet of the 1950s and 1960s who helped define the sound of Motown. They even featured a jazzed-up version of R2-D2, the astromech droid robot character featured in the movie Star Wars. In this 30-second clip the robot named George is called into the room and he asks, "What's the fuss Gus?" and he tells the beautiful woman to "Change the pace, Grace!" and my favorite, "You are so right, Dwight!" The ad ends with reassurance from the crew by letting the viewers know, "It's nice to know that in the future you will still be able to get malt liquor in outer space." The commercials not only glamourized their product, but the message that I was receiving was one of success, immortality, and most of all, fun...and that is all I wanted, a lot of fun.

It was reassuring to know that my drink of choice would be available anywhere in the universe, because I was getting deeper into music and George Clinton and his Parliament-Funkadelic funk mob promised me that space is where we as people were headed and I wanted to ride. Thousands have written about the band who was inducted into the rock and Roll Hall of Fame in May 1997. *Rolling Stone* magazine ranked the band number 56 on the list of the 100 greatest bands of all time. But PBS.org's summation says it all when the author writes, "Clinton's music created an alternate universe of 'aliens' bringing the redemptive power of funk to a world sorely in need of a new point of view." The Motown sound had my respect, but this was something new, something raw, something sinister and more important--they sang about drugs and the need to be free.

Let me be crystal clear, I did realize that they were not the first group to sing about the pleasure of drugs. There were scores of rock acts that beat Clinton to the punch in that arena. But no one had ever created characters and themes. The Motor Booty Affair Album is just one shining example of his creative genius. The tag line for the album and the concert tour was "Where you can dance underwater and not get wet." The characters were on a mission to raise the lost city of Atlantis from the bottom of the sea by music and dance--or in George's own words, "We're gonna raise Atlantis to the top with the bump and the bop." This fish tale included villains and heroines with names like Charlie Tuna, Rita the Mermaid, and Sir Nose D'void of Funk, who vowed that he was too cool to swim because he might get his hair wet.

The jacket on the inside of the album showed a smiling Clinton riding two dolphins down Bimini Way dressed in a white cowboy outfit, red bandana around his neck, ten-gallon hat, and white shaggy fur chaps, steadying a boom box to one ear with his right hand and holding the reins to the dolphins with his left hand. There is a wake behind him like jet skis of today would leave, he is smiling--and just like he promised, he is not wet! The last song on the album is entitled "Deep." This is another" long song" that goes on for over ten minutes, and in this Funk masterpiece the listener is reminded, "You can lead a horse to water but you can't make him backstroke or snort coke." The local radio stations were reluctant to play his music.

Censorship was at its zenith, so acts like Clinton would produce what I would like to call "radio jams." These songs were usually three to four minutes long (album versions could last up to twenty minutes in length) and were "cleaned up" to make the playlist. I would do odd jobs around our neighborhood to earn enough money to secure the albums. I would walk around school singing songs like "America Eats Its Young" and "I'm Feeling Better by the Pound."

This stuff was raw like sushi and I craved it more and more. Cutting-edge high-powered amplifiers, pre-amps, and sound equalizers were the rage. The bigger the equipment, the more power and watts per channel it delivered. Watts per channel simply identifies how much power the source can supply to each speaker. Cerwin Vega, Yamaha, Denon, and JBL were some of the industry leaders that set the bar on the level of system that one owned. My brother Charles was in high school and working part time as a check processor for a local bank downtown. He invested in a huge set of realistic speakers, powered by a Denon 100 watt per channel amplifier, and a Technics turntable manufactured by Panasonic that was equipped with an Audio Technica cartridge with a diamond-tipped stylus. The cartridge and stylus played an integral part in the stereo separation, sound clarity, and deep bass that we were trying to achieve with the system. A Denon Cassette Deck was used to record our magic and take it on the road and we brought it all to life with a Realistic equalizer that had a built-in reverberator on it. This system slammed!

I applied to be our local paperboy. I was interviewed for the job and I was awarded the job of delivering the *Jacksonville Journal*. The now-defunct gazette began its publication as the *Metropolis* in the early 1900s and was renamed the *Jacksonville Journal* in 1922. The *Journal* was historically weaker than our morning newspaper (*The Florida Times Union*) and published only Monday-Friday. Although it had a smaller circulation, the *Journal* had its moments in the 1960s. The *Journal* was a plucky younger sister to the *Times Union* in the '70s and '80s. The job was simple. Each day the branch manager would drop off bundles of the afternoon periodical to my home, and all I had to do was deliver them to the subscribers' homes in a timely manner. I was given a big, heavy white sack that resembled burlap with the word JOURNAL emblazoned in blue oversized letters on the front of it. The bag had thick straps on each side deigned to be wrapped around the handlebars of a bicycle. Under the guise of saving for college tuition money, the income generated from my first job was used primarily to fund my lifestyle. I would buy an occasional shirt, pair of pants, or school supplies to keep my parents off the scent, but the bulk went to alcohol, drugs, and albums. I could make anywhere from $25 to $125 a week in my new position. This fueled my thirst for my party life and like any good friend would do I brought Laurence along for the ride. With my newfound bounty the partying was happening more frequently and more intense. The quarts of beer were being replaced by six-packs. The 7- cent bags of weed were shunned for the 25-cent bags of weed.

My mother was as proud of me having that job as I was having it. She helped me in every way possible to maintain the part-time gig that was taking up more of my time than I had imagined. There were days when she would add the advertisements into the main body of the paper for me. These came in separate bundles and had to be hand stuffed into the newspaper. On rainy days she would fold them then insert the papers into plastic bags to prevent them from becoming wet as I slung them from one side of the street to the other. On cold and extremely rainy days she would load me into the car and she would drive me on the small but demanding route.

At the time, my brother Joe was away serving our country in the United States Navy. He had purchased a snowflake-white 1977 6.6 liter Pontiac Trans Am before serving his tour of duty. The muscle car was equipped with dual exhaust, and a beautiful fish scale dashboard which included a tachometer and oil pressure gauges staring you in the face. It had a scarlet-red interior with bucket seats and a console. The steering wheel was a small thick sphere with honeycomb webbing with a red phoenix in the center. My brother ordered the car without the signature bird on the hood but it did have the "shaker" hood. The air intake extended through an opening in the hood and when the car came to life it would shake impressively as the V8 225hp Buick engine rumbled. It had rectangular headlights and a flat black grill that gave the car a mean, mysterious look. The car was built low to the ground and was one of the first cars that I had seen with flared fenders, and spoilers that were designed to keep the car from taking flight. My mother would load me and those papers into his prized sports car and away we would go to deliver the evening news. I am sure she was uncomfortable driving the car and felt guilty using my brother's prize possession for such a task, but she would do anything for her babies.

Helping is doing something for someone that is not capable of doing himself, and enabling is doing for someone things that he could and should be doing himself, writes Allison Bottke, author of *Setting Boundaries for Your Children*. Any attempt at describing my mother's love for us would be inadequate and lacking. I am sure there are physiological and genetic reasons that are mixed in the equation, but my mother's love was best expressed in the feeling that I got from seeing her, sharing my thoughts with her, or just hearing the sweet calming sound of her voice. She was caring and compassionate, stern but sweet, demanding yet divine. The best word--and there are many--to describe my mama is "angelic." What usually starts out as helping ends up crippling the individual and leads to enabling. I was no exception to this rule, and as you will read later in the book how many who thought they were helping, fueled decades of enabling.

I began my ninth-grade school year with high expectations on the basketball court as well as the classroom. I was the only eighth-grader grader to play and start on the varsity team the previous year. I was hyped to be the Magic Johnson or Larry Bird of the mighty Patriots. I accepted the challenge and also the notoriety, fame, girls, and other fringe benefits that came with the honor. My paper route gig was booming and I had money for the latest menswear, which included an array of different-colored Swedish Knit dress pants--these were impressive shiny, knit ranch-style pants in style at the time that featured authentic western styling, flared pant legs with a flattering appearance, and only the upper echelon in urban men's fashions were privy to their wares. They were usually paired with a "knick knick," a polyester button-down wild, vivid shirt with colorful patterns. The patterns ranged from a bulldog shooting pool in a billiards hall to a naked lady with huge gold hoop earrings sporting a huge Afro. The entire ensemble, no matter which shirt you chose, was extremely flammable and prone to accidental burns--as witnessed by some, including me, who had "seed holes" in the crotch area of the pants permanently scarred by the popping out of very hot marijuana seeds when the pot was not "cleaned" properly. The seeds would literally ignite and pop out of the "joint" like Orville Redenbacher popcorn kernels in a hot skillet and go through those pants like a hot knife through butter. If you had those signature holes in your pants, everybody from the pimp to the preacher knew how they got there.

My shoe size had skyrocketed to a size twelve so I could wear my older brother's and my dad's shoes, so I had a plethora of styles to choose from to complement my outfits. Wearing athletic shoes to school was not considered cool at the time; they were packed in your gym bag and used exclusively for

Physical Education class or for practice. NIKE was new to the world of athletic shoes; leather was introduced and was fast replacing the canvas-style Chuck Taylor that had monopolized the sport shoe industry for decades. I purchased my first pair of blue-and-white NIKEs for the upcoming season. They were a size twelve leather, low top with the familiar NIKE swoosh and the original footwear to have the US size and the UK size on the inside of the tongue of the shoe.

I was the perennial favorite to be the MVP and leading scorer for that year's team. We were not favored to win the championship, but were predicted to have a modest season and make it to the playoffs. My basketball skills were diminishing due to lack of preparation, lack of interest, and drinking. Although I was not voted MVP for the basketball team, I was voted Most Likely to Succeed--along with Denise Kornegay one of the smartest kids in the school. I figured one out of two isn't bad, and my justification for not getting the sports award was due to my putting in more time in my studies. Well, the fact of the matter is intelligence came to me naturally because of my parents' involvement, the need to be considered intelligent, and seeing education as a rite of passage. Conversely, sports involved more preparation, conditioning, and practice, all of which was taking a backseat to my self-destructive lifestyle.

The summer of 1979 was upon me and I had plans to come into basketball season in better shape and to improve my basic fundamentals. I knew that my skills were diminishing instead of improving, so a steady regimen of calisthenics, conditioning, and practice was all I needed. My grades were at an all-time high, so I had no plans to do anything differently in the classroom. I would be going to the south side of town and attending Sandalwood Senior High to become a fighting saint. The school had been built in 1971 and was regarded as an engineering marvel. My brothers Russell, James, Joe, and Charles had graduated in 1973, '74, '75, and '79, so the Preston name was well known.

I rode bus number 348 and on the first day of school a girl named Monica had saved me a seat on the crowded bus and sought me out by name and insisted that I sit by her which I obliged. She had on a lot of makeup and sported red curly hair. She was very aggressive toward me, almost claiming me as I sat down next to her. I was a tad puzzled, a bit perplexed but pleased to have the attention of the opposite sex. She was a senior, three years older than me, a cougar by definition since I was fifteen and she was old enough to drive, fight for her country, and buy alcohol, the last of which was the most impressive. Although it was comforting to have female companionship established, the person that I was looking forward to meeting the most did not wear a skirt, have long eyelashes, or sport bright ruby red lips. My brother Charles had told me stories of a Sandalwood legend: a man who always sat on the back of the bus reveling in his thoughts. A man revered for his coolness and consistency, a man who not only smoked the finest weed but smoked it on the bus. Hallelujah!

As I scanned my new surroundings with Monica questioning me about everything from my shoe size to my dreams in life, I looked for the urban legend...Tony. I interrupted Monica and asked her to point him out to me. With a somewhat bewildered look on her face, she informed me that he got on at the last stop. Monica was now talking so much it had become annoying, but she smelled good and she was pretty so I just grinned and bore it. When we approached the last stop I peered through the small rectangular windows of the yellow Bluebird as the bus came to a halt. A single-file line formed and I quickly assessed my new peers.

Before I could go through the lineup on my own, Monica blurted out, "That's Tony." He was not what I had expected. I had envisioned a rough, gruff, tough hombre. He just looked average--tall, medium build and an Afro smothered by a Frankie Beverly-style cap. He had a blue windbreaker on, with a morning newspaper tucked under his arm. He entered the bus and like most of the seniors, he looked around as if to evaluate the incoming sophomore class. I made brief eye contact, careful not to stare at the mythical man whom I admired before I had even met him. He gave me a nod of the head as he passed by our seat. Monica was still talking but whatever she was saying, I definitely was not listening now. He went to the back of the bus and took his seat, which had been reserved although the bus was at near capacity before arriving at the stop.

The bus lurched forward as the bus driver came off of the clutch a little too fast. The bus merged onto Interstate 95 and we were on our way. The route would take us east on the 20th Street Expressway and around Dead Man's Curve, a banked curve on the thoroughfare that resembled the banked walls at the Daytona International Speedway. Instead of taking the Matthews Bridge as I did in elementary school, we would now be going over the Isaiah D. Hart Bridge. As we headed toward our destination, I smelled it. The faint trace of high grade marijuana was permeating my nostrils. This was no Yeti, Bigfoot, or Loch Ness monster sighting—this urban legend was true and I was experiencing it. Moments later, the magic happened. Tony walked up to where I was sitting and asked me if I would like to join him. We smoked but never talked--you don't talk to a legend. We finished the joint a few miles before arriving at our destination.

The school itself was huge. It covered five acres under one roof. The transition from my old junior high's gym to this state-of-the-art field house would best be described as going from that old rickety basketball rim that we erected on 24th street to Madison Square Garden. I was welcomed as a much-needed addition to the team from the ninth-grade basketball team's incumbents that were looking forward to having a winning junior varsity team.

Kyle Dean, the tallest player on our team, greeted me and welcomed me with great exuberance. Kyle stood about 6 feet 5 inches and was as thin as a sheet of paper held side-ways. Kyle drove an orange Volkswagen Beetle that sported a Florida vanity plate with the words "K- Dean" scrolled across the back. As we talked, we realized that we had a lot in com-mon. He grew up on the "other side" of the expressway, and although we didn't attend the same elementary and junior high schools, we had familiar friends. Kyle's mother was an educator, a librarian who would later write *An African Beach for African-Americans*.

The first time I was introduced to Marsha Dean-Phelts she did a double take when her son said my surname. Mrs. Dean-Phelts was opening her mail and when she heard that name she peered over her stereotypical librarian-style glasses complete with a chain holding them steadily around her neck and exclaimed, "Are you related to the Prestons off of Grothe Street?"

I responded proudly, "Yes, ma'am!"

I earned instant credibility for being the grandson of one of the most respected men in the community. My paternal grandfather was good friends with A. Phillip Randolph, a leader in the African-American civil rights movement. He organized and led the brotherhood of sleeping car porters, the first predominantly black labor union in the country. Although we had grown up within walking distance of one another's home, I had never met him before our introduction at Sandalwood. Kyle filled me in on the coach that I would be playing for and what would be expected of me as a new member of the Sandalwood Saints. My interest in basketball was decreasing daily, like the brightness of a waning moon. I needed to know if Kyle drank, did he smoke weed, how was he with the girls-these would be the ultimate common interests that would initiate a friendship.

I made the team and a starting position on the junior varsity team. My work ethic was at a standstill. I gave the minimum amount of effort just to stay even, never thinking about improving my ball-handling abilities, or my jump shot and endurance. I was however making huge strides in drinking and partying. I was sitting next to Tony on the thirty-minute ride to school and I was smoking pot on a daily basis. I maintained a very high grade point average. I understood that I had a better chance of making it to college with my brain than with my brawn. Let's just face it, I hadn't grown an inch since seventh grade and was now considered one of the little guys on the court, and I had not adapted my game to fit my lack of height.

I couldn't dribble in a crowd or shoot very well from the perimeter. These are skills that I could have been sharpened with the immortal words of one Allen Iverson, "practice."

Halfway through the season, I earned the right to operate a motor vehicle in the state of Florida. As a reward for keeping his car clean and obtaining a driver's license, my brother Charles agreed to let me have the car for the first time all to myself. Charles trusted me with his new 1980 Chevrolet Monza. It was beige in color and had one of those sunroofs that could easily be propped up--or with a little effort it could be completely removed and stored in its own black vinyl carrying case. The car had rims the same color of the car and a slot-style grill and came equipped Chevrolet's new 4.3-liter V-8 engine that was manufactured to compete with the Ford Mustang II and other sports coupes.

The AM-FM Delco radio that came as standard equipment never made it to our house. On the way home from John Deihl Chevrolet we stopped at The House of Stereo and purchased an Alpine AM-FM cassette deck and graphic equalizer (power booster) and had them installed along with a pair of Jensen 6x9 coaxial speakers. This system delivered over 100 watts per channel and the equalizer enhanced the frequencies of the sound. In other words, it was used to bring out the full-frequency spectrum of the musical performance. It improved clarity and spatial separation, allowing the listener to hear every instrument and voice.

In fact, when I was taking my road test for my driver's license, the instructor was so inquisitive about the apparatus that was bolted to the passenger's side of the console, we pulled over and I explained how everything worked. The song was Ray Parker and Raydio's "Rock On." I let her listen to it with the amp off, then I turned it on and the music went from good to hey Ray's in the car. The windows vibrated and the floorboard shook as the musicians shouted like their lives depended on it. I fast forwarded the tape to my favorite of the album, "Hot Stuff." This nasty up tempo jam starts out with the guitar player playing a funky rhythm and is soon joined by a thunderous bass that symbolizes funk at its best. The Department of Motor Vehicle employee was in a musical hypnosis as she tapped her rose-colored fingernails on her clipboard and rolled her neck to the thumping sound of the music. After a few minutes of the tune, she gathered herself and told me to signal, look over my left shoulder and proceed. As I reached for the volume control she put her hand over mine as if to say, "Don't you dare." The gesture was implied and I got the message.

We turned a few corners and jammed, she motioned for me to return to the office and park. I asked the obvious question and she replied, "Child, you know you passed! And how do I get my car to sound like this?"

We were scheduled to play the Fletcher Senators, a rival school located in nearby Neptune Beach. The day started out like so many other days had become, smoking dope and drinking in the morning, attending class during the day, followed by family life at home in the evenings. I was beginning to live a double life. After handing me the keys to his car and handing out a few warnings about everything from speeding to smoking in his car, I opened the car door, slid into the cockpit, adjusted the seats and mirrors, put in a cassette that I had recorded for the occasion that included a compilation of funk. I utilized all the skills that I had learned while studying to get my coveted license and carefully headed to the game.

The game was uneventful and we won, to the delight of the small crowd that had come out to see us play on a Friday night. The varsity team always played after our games had concluded and typically we would gather to cheer them on. This night there would be no cheering the team on, because usually if we were at an away game we would have to ride the bus back to our gym only to be taken home by awaiting parents or some other responsible adult, and games played at home were overseen and managed by faculty and other coaches. I made the assertion that this victory must be celebrated. After all, my birthday had just passed, I'd had a victory on the court, and most of all there was the need to hallow one more piece of freedom in my life. There was a tidal wave of mysticism raging in the young age generation called me.

The party started at the rear of the car with me popping the hatchback and blasting the music. The girls started to accumulate as I played more music. This party called for a more radio-friendly style of music--the kind with the catchy riffs and choruses that let them laugh, sing, and shake what they mama gave them. The Gap band's "You Dropped a Bomb on Me" and "Burn Rubber" were songs that always got the girls shaking their groove thing. This was not the time for my main man Mr. Clinton to hit us with any of his "psychoalphadiscobetabioaquadoloops" I needed to keep pumping dance music.

Three members of the basketball team--Ben Lundy, James McMiller, and Kyle Dean-- joined me in my spontaneous outdoor parking lot party. Ben was the point guard on the team, a small cheerful fellow with chubby cheeks and a grin as wide as the Grand Canyon. He was a southpaw and had a quick, first step that reminded you of the Boston Celtic's Nate "Tiny" Archibald. He had always admired and respected me and was considered one of my best friends. James was a forward on the team. James was best known for his well-groomed Afro and his red Chevrolet Monte Carlo. Unlike the rest of us knuckle-heads, James was mature far beyond his years. He was quiet and unassuming, dressed conservatively, and was always on the honor roll. Kyle was the center on our team. He was 6 foot 5 inches tall and was mischievous (not in a bad way) and private. Dean never wore his thoughts on his sleeve. If you really wanted to know what was on his mind you would have to poke and prod to get to the real concern.

We had four distinct personalities that drew us close to-gether like astronauts in the World Space Station. Four mem-bers of the cheerleading squad had made their way over to the impromptu bash. Michelle, Caroline, Sandi, and Renise were all members of the junior varsity cheerleading squad. Michelle's parents owned the local skate boarding rink called Kona. Michelle was a short, curvaceous brunette with curly hair and a wit that reminded you of Phyllis Diller. Caroline was the naïve little sister that I never had. She had a sanguine personality. The beautiful squad leader was naturally cheer-ful and displayed vast amounts of social interest and energy. Caroline was exuberant, enthusiastic, and expansive. Renise was on the opposite end of the spectrum. She was more laid back and seemed to rely on others to lead the way. She had the body of today's supermodels. She stood over 5'-11" tall and was thin, very attractive, sexy, and stunning.

Sandra was my high school sweetheart. She was arguably

the most popular black girl in the sophomore class when I arrived at Sandalwood. She was the catch that every guy wanted to land. She had lovely milk-chocolate-colored skin and a personality that attracted me like a magnet to steel. Although we were both African-American, Sandi and I came from two different worlds. She had grown up just a stone's throw away from school in what was then considered one of the nicest subdivisions east of the St. John's River, called Beachwood. I was as unfamiliar to her as she was to me, but she was the most popular black girl in our class and I was the most popular black guy in our class. We were determined to make it work.

After dancing and hanging out at the car, yours truly wanted to introduce some real fun into the equation. I had figured out by now that a tipsy girl was a girl that did not always make the best choices and a drunken girl was ripe for the picking. We all agreed that a little spirits would liven up the party.

The guys hopped into the car with me and we made a beeline to the closest convenience store. It was located at the entrance into Beachwood. I boldly went inside and made my selection of Schlitz malt liquor bull in quart sizes, paid for the items, and drove back to the school to covertly drink in the parking lot. The Alcohol Epidemiology Program at the University of Minnesota is a study entitled Youth Access to Alcohol. The study involved over 6000 teenagers and revealed that boys were more likely to buy alcohol from a store, bar, or restaurant and convenience stores are the easiest place to buy it. The study goes on to say most believed they would not face serious legal consequences from drinking. We were batting a thousand at that moment. We returned with the drinks and continued to party like it was 1999.

The school employed a security officer that lived in a trailer on the grounds of the school. His name was Mr. Adams. He was a middle-aged balding man with a passion and knack for catching teenagers doing something wrong. He seemed to always show up when you least expected him—tonight would be no different. We had assigned monitors to be on the lookout for old Hawkeye Adams, as we used to call him, but as we got more intoxicated our inhibitions increased and our judgment decreased. We would spot him and then turn the music down and put the party favors away for periods at a time. But because we were so inebriated by now the option of going inside to enjoy the rest of the game was not a viable one anymore. We stayed our course and partied literally to the bitter end.

The game finally ended and as were winding down our parking lot bash, out of nowhere a directional projection of light energy radiated from some form of light source. I looked up to see if it was coming from the courtesy light inside of the car that automatically comes on when one of the doors is ajar, or maybe it was the street lights in the parking lot being deflected and passing obliquely through my windshield...or could it have been the light of the moon trickling down from the bleeding sky? No, the light source was emanating from Adams' long, black-handled service-issue flashlight that also doubled as a billy club. The beam of light illuminated the inside of the car like fireworks on the 4th of July. He shined the blinding light in my face and ordered me to remove the keys from the ignition. My short life passed before my eyes. I saw glimpses of my mother, father and my trusting brother. How could I have been so foolish?

Adams barked, "Everybody out of the car!" We scrambled out of the car like clowns out of a circus car. The security officer reached in and started to pull out our belongings, warm-up jackets, wristbands, knee pads, pom-poms…then he hit pay dirt. He reached underneath the driver's seat and found a half-empty bottle of malt liquor…and no, it was not half full because at this moment, I was a pessimist. He lined us up against the school as he started his "investigation." As he searched the car, we had an opportunity to converse and formulate a somewhat plausible explanation for eight eighteen-year-olds to be drinking alcohol on school property. Even Johnny Cochran couldn't have saved us from the fate that inevitably headed our way. Like any well-trained officer of the law, he interviewed the girls first to get the truth and the boys last to see just how much we were going to lie. Much to my delight, we were not detained for long. After writing down statements, we were free to go on our merry way. Thinking that we had dodged the proverbial bullet, we stopped on the way home and got more beer to celebrate the narrow escape. In our small naïve minds, we were under the assertion that if old Adams didn't see us take a drink out of that bottle, then he had no case.

During the weekend, the incident stayed on my mind. I had sobered up and undoubtedly felt terrible, scared and uneasy about what had transpired on Friday night. I could sense that my mother knew something wasn't quite right with me. When I arrived at the bus stop the following Monday, I didn't drink a beer, which was quickly picked up on by my peers. Meanwhile the daily ritual of smoking a joint with Tony Long was passed up as well. I figured that I might be called into the office to explain things further, so being sober just might be a good thing. The day was going without incident. We all tried to limit the discussion on the night in question to try to minimize or diffuse the tangled web that we had woven for ourselves.

We made it through our first class of the day, then on to homeroom. This was the class where students were counted either present or absent for the day and all announcements were made over the school's intercom system. Suddenly, the door opened. It was the representative from the Dean of Boys' office with a white slip of paper in his hand. He approached my teacher, Mrs. Sisler, and handed it to her and tried not to look in my direction. My heart sank even before she called my name, "Richard, you are needed in the office," she calmly said.

As I walked with the aide who I had never given the time of day to, I asked him if he knew why I was summoned to Dean Hayes' office, and like a good dedicated servant of school discipline, he took the fifth. The office was located hundreds of yards from my homeroom, but it was as if we sprinted there in world-record time. I was led to a room that I had never seen before, and when the door was opened I was led in, and much to my chagrin I was seated next to my co-defendants. Kyle motioned for me to look over at a small table located in the corner of the room. My eyes could not believe what I saw. Located on the top of the rhombus-shaped walnut veneer table was Exhibit A, the confiscated half-empty bottle of premium malt liquor. I had never felt so helpless in my life. The gravity of the situation was pulling together bodies with forces directly proportional to the offense that we had committed. One by one we were led away to give us one last chance to explain the situation. In my case, it was a futile attempt to reverse the inevitable, like throwing water on a core meltdown of a nuclear reactor. We were all deemed guilty. The only thing to decide now was the sentence for the crime.

Dean Hayes was a tall man with red curly hair who resembled Bill Walton, the "big redhead" who won college basketball player of the year three times while playing for UCLA in the seventies. He had a raspy voice that came from years of smoking Marlboro Reds. While we were imagining being suspended for a matter of days, the administration had something else in mind. Hayes had netted a cascade of big fish. Michelle was our class president, James was in the top 5 percent of our class academically, Renise's mother was a teacher at the school, Sandi and Caroline was the darlings of the 10th grade, Ben was the jovial high-spirited student that everyone liked, and then there was me, an evolving master alcoholic progressively getting more involved with drugs and alcohol… a young man on a one-way street destined for heartache, disappointment and failure.

I was well aware that the punishment for the offense was not going to be a slap on the wrist; after all we were all first offenders, and we were officers and athletes in the school. We all had impeccable records and were among the most-liked students in the school. We were all well-respected by our teachers and the administration. After reviewing all of this, surely they would understand the quality of students that we were and take all of that into consideration before making a ruling. But what we had failed to realize was The Duval

County School Board had recently enacted a Student Code of Conduct. It was written that this jurisdiction of the board was in effect during the school day and at regular school-sponsored activities, while being transported on school buses or at public expense to and from school or other educational activities, at all times and places, including, but not limited to, school-sponsored events, field trips, athletic functions, and other activities where appropriate school personnel have jurisdiction over students. It went on to say that all school regulations and prohibitions pertained to automobiles driven or parked on school property. Yikes!

We were all given a copy of the document with our parents' signature on it as well as ours. The situation was that had started out like harmless fun was now snowballing out of control like a racing car with no brakes. We were all summoned into the office one by one to learn our fate. The girls went first and each of them left the office in hysteria I had only witnessed at funerals. As Ben, Kyle, and James exited the office the looks on their faces were ones of confusion, dismay, and disbelief. I was still optimistic that I could explain the situation one last time, have them see it my way, and once again Richard Preston would emerge from all of this and somehow save the day. When my name was called, I stood up and smoothed out the creases in my Levi's, tucked my shirt neatly in my pants, held my head high, and entered the room.

Shockingly, Hayes passed the phone to me and simply said, "Someone would like to speak to you." I cleared my throat, stood erect, smoothed my pants, and made sure that my shirt was tucked in all the way. The voice on the other end of the phone was the voice that I had heard since being in the womb, the loving voice that had sang to me countless nights as a child, the voice that had instructed me on how to be the best that I could be, the voice that prayed for me in my time of need, the voice that was sweeter than any sugar, molasses, or honey.

She was direct and to the point. "You have really stepped in the mess this time, haven't you?"

"What are you talking about?" I retorted.

"Richard, do you realize that you have been expelled?"

I replied with the best song-and-dance show that I could put together in the spur of the moment. I blamed everyone from Jim Crow to President Jimmy Carter--and besides, they were just bluffing to get me to talk. The jailhouse lawyer in me had us facing 3-5 day suspensions max. There was no way that the administration would suspend the upper echelon of the class--for God's sake, the class president couldn't be expelled, could she? We were, after all, model students in a model school. These types of things happened on the other side of town, not in our pristine paradise called Sandalwood. A hand touched my shoulder as if to say "Your time is up." I said a confident goodbye to my mother and placed the placed the cream-colored phone with the row of flashing lights on the bottom to designate different phone lines and the red one at the end to place lines on hold back to its resting spot on the desk.

I was about to sit down when Dean Hayes said, "Go empty out your locker, collect all of your school-issued textbooks and return them to me. You have five minutes to complete this task and leave the campus, or you will be considered trespassing on school property and escorted off by the Jacksonville Sherriff's Office."

Was this really happening to us? After all, we were not some uneducated, trouble- causing riff raff that had somehow suddenly materialized out of thin air; we had purpose, meaning, and loyalty. We were the good guys, we wore white, we came to save the day...surely there were others worthy of an expulsion. The smokers in the boys' room, the ones that habitually skipped school, the girls who performed oral sex under the bleachers, the ones who didn't care, these are the individuals that you should go after--not us. This terrible day was happening at warp speed. I was waiting for Allen Funt to come out of nowhere and yell "Smile, you are on *Candid Camera*" --the original practical joke/reality series that featured ordinary people being confronted with unusual situations.

I arrived at locker number 756 and began to rotate the blue dial on the school-issued Master lock, 32 to the right, 16 to the left, and back to 23. The lock dropped open with a thud and so did the large lump in my throat. I removed the geometry book and the physics book from their perch; next I removed the basketball schedule that I had taped to the locker door. The Algebra 2 book, the English composition and Spanish book all had to be turned in immediately to the administration. The extraction was taking place during class time, so I was able to move about clandestinely and keep questions to a minimum. I scurried back to the office with the books and placed them on Hayes' desk.

I was then given a document outlining the punishment. I was going to be going to an alternative school for forty-five days; this school, Darnell-Cookman, was designated for students who had committed a Class 3 offense. These offenses were not your garden variety, run-of-the- mill student situations, but felonious acts that in today's climate warrant jail time. They included, but were not limited to, bringing weapons on school property, having sexual relations on school grounds, assaulting the staff--and yes, consumption of alcohol and/or drugs on school property. If Sandalwood was a pearl, this school was a rock. It was located in the heart of the inner city. It was two blocks north of one of the most notorious projects in the city. The alternative learning center had a drive-thru liquor store across the street, and Jacksonville's largest trauma hospital was a stone's throw from the principal's office. We said goodbye to the lush lawns of the Southside and said hello to the hard pounding of asphalt and concrete.

We arrived at the facility while the nine-week grading system was in progress. We jumped right on board like a hobo hitching a freight train out of the rail yard; there were no formal introductions, no syllabuses were handed out, no orientations were extended to the eight clean-cut students from the Southside school. You literally had to "get in where you fit in" or this bad dream was going to become a nine-week, nauseating nightmare. James, Ben, Kyle, and I grew up not far from the school, so although we didn't hang around the general population of Darnell-Cookman, we were aware that they existed. Conversely, the girls were not as fortunate in that sense, so it was going to be a struggle to adapt to such harsh, crass, disrespectful individuals.

A large percentage of these young adults--and in some cases, adults--were troubled beyond the capabilities of a fix from an education center. We quickly ascertained that some were illiterate, sexually abused, and dysfunctional. I vividly recall one day in our English class we were given a scrambled set of words on the chalkboard and asked to construct a sentence out of those words. Curt, who had come from a rival Northside school, Jean Ribault, and who was serving his time for selling cocaine on school premises put together a gem of a sentence for class discussion. "One snow-covered France" was what he came up with from that assignment, and the rest is alternative school history.

We quickly became an enigma in a world of retribution and reform. Students, administrators, and even the custodians would do a double take when they would see us and all had the look of "one of these things is not like the other, one of these things just doesn't belong" the well-known skit that was seen on *Sesame Street* for decades. On the exterior perhaps I was different, but deep inside I was probably more jaded than the rest of my constituents. Unable to realize it at the time, I was allowing a mood-altering substance to interfere with my normal activities. My new God was drugs and alcohol; my life was becoming unmanageable…but of course I had nothing to do with my circumstances. I would chalk it all up to bad luck, bad timing, and bad planning. I had no intention of assessing the negligence before addressing the need. My inability to digest what was happening to me left me vulnerable to a world that had chewed me up and spit out men far wiser, richer and spiritual than this hormone-raging sixteen-year-old kid. We did our "sentence" but always felt that we committed no crime. The return to our "normal" school went well and of course there were questions to be answered and stories to be told about life away from our tranquil sanctum.

My junior year began and I picked up where I left off in most aspects of my life. The big change was that sports were now over. I had lost interest in participating, but the fact was my skills were gone, I was not growing anymore, and the fact that I would rather party than practice made that decision as easy as choosing which floor to choose in an elevator of a two-story building. I had landed a job at the largest fast food chain in America. Most of the restaurants in the neighborhood were family-owned specialty diners, dives, and good old-fashioned hole in the walls. I fell in love with the job. We watched training videos, our uniforms had to be neatly pressed, and I was afforded the opportunity to work next to women and get a steady paycheck every other Friday.

Once again I had convinced my parents to let me have the job to help out with my upcoming college expenses. I tried to convince myself that the money would go to that single purpose as well but in reality, it was fuel thrown on a fire that was rapidly getting out of control. I was becoming consumed and obsessed with getting messed up. I found myself going to seedier places, taking unnecessary risks, and hanging out with the "wrong" crowd. While loved ones condemned my actions, I viewed them as new chapters in my life--adventure and exploration. After all, I had been raised to not judge anyone, so I rationalized all of this in my bright but not- so-clear mind.

My drinking and dope smoking escalated in leaps and bounds when I accepted that job. Most of my fellow co-workers were out of high school and into the life that I was seeking. The neighborhood liquor store was in plain view as we cooked burgers, fried fish fillets, and swirled sundaes. We would all put our funds together each day and thirty minutes before closing our store we would designate a willing participant to make the "run" to procure the party favors. After walking the last customer to the door and securing the doors, the place was transformed to nightclub slash dope emporium. The Muzak system that earlier in the day was playing the tranquil sounds of Tony Bennett and Frank Sinatra were replaced with Prince, Morris Day, and the Time and all the funky hits of that era. The ice machine was now stocked with our favorite malt liquors, with Mickey's Malt and Private Stock malt beverages leading the way. For the folks who had to clean the lobby area we made their task easier and more enjoyable by filling empty five-gallon pickle buckets with ice. These served as portable coolers to be placed strategically throughout the restaurant for ease and convenience.

Cleaning up the restaurant, sanitizing the literally hundreds of parts in the ice cream and shake machines, draining the gallons of shortening out of the frying vats and filtering its contents, washing the dishes and counting the inventory was suddenly transformed from labor to leisure and relaxation thanks to my crutch that I so heavily depended on now. I was also becoming hooked on the sub-status-quo culture and the lifestyle that it represented. I was always careful to portray myself as something of a rebel, being sympathetic to the ones whose education, values, and socioeconomic status were different from what I had grown to know. The "golden arches" stood just blocks from one the poorest neighborhoods in Jacksonville at that time illuminating success over despair. Many of the employees were either living in the Blodgett Homes or in its midst far away from the lower-middle-class environment in which I was reared. I was a functioning addict, a babe in addiction if you will, and very interested in furthering my education.

Like many of my peers, I applied for a plethora of college scholarships and grants. My father and I would clear the dining room table at the house and fill out endless applications for financial assistance to help with school. I had the grades and the test scores to go to most major universities in the country, and by Jove he was going to see me through to the very end. My father was tough, but looking back he was trying to produce the best product society had to offer when it came to his boys. After submitting each application, we would anxiously await the replies. "A mind is a terrible thing to waste" was the motto of the United Negro College Fund. I had scored very well on the on my college boards.

I remember taking the Scholastic Aptitude Test (SAT) at Edward Waters College, a predominantly black college located off Kings Road in the New Town area of Jacksonville. The SAT is a suite of tools to assess your readiness for college. This exam provides a path to opportunities and financial-supported scholarships in a way that is supposed to be fair to all students. The morning of the test I had a hangover from a night of partying. Although I knew the importance of doing well on this test, I drank smoked weed and danced into the wee hours of the night. I was so hung over that I had to have a drink that morning just to make it to the campus. Nevertheless, I ended up scoring a 1460 on the test. If you are not familiar with the scoring of this test, a perfect score is 1600.

I would come home each day and ask my mom if "it" had arrived. The "it" that I was referring to was replies from one of the many applications that my father and I had submitted. I was earnestly looking forward to attending college, obtaining a degree, being a thriving, productive member of society and living happily ever after, as the story goes. I longed to attend an out-of-city school but I was coming to the realization that without the help of the money that I was supposed to be saving, I would be probably have to stay in town and live at home to reduce costs as much as possible.

The letter arrived: "Congratulations on your acceptance into our undergrad program at Jacksonville University," the letter read. J. U. was a private college located in the Arlington section of town, shaded by overgrown oaks built on the banks of the St. Johns River. It had an enrollment of fewer than 3,000 students at that time, a renowned mathematics department, and a student union building that served beer on campus. Sign me up. There was just one little hitch in the whole deal--the scholarship that I was awarded was N.R.O.T.C. scholarship. In The Naval Reserve Officers Training Corps, midshipmen, as we were called, are required to complete the course of study prescribed by the college or university that they attend. Midshipmen are also required to take several naval science courses in addition to their college prescribed course load.

An officer in the Navy would fit me just fine. I did not know much about them, but from the images I got from television, they seemed really cool. They drank, had power, and wore cool uniforms. Besides, my father had been in the Navy in World War II and served proudly in a segregated Navy where, once drafted, he wasn't even allowed to sleep in a sleeping car on a train ride from Florida to Seattle because he was a black man. In my mind, I would avenge the atrocities imposed on my dad and would rise and lead the very souls that treated him like a second class citizen. I had it all planned in my head, but unlike my father some forty years earlier who was held down by another man's ignorance, I was holding myself down due to my own ignorance and it came not through demeaning names, oppression, and hate, but in a bottle. I was beginning to rust from the inside out. My frame was as sturdy as the Eiffel Tower, but my infrastructure was in need of repair.

CHAPTER 4
Frying Pan to the Fire

In an article written by Caleb Hellerman for *CNN Health* in 2011, the author writes, long before drug cartels, crack wars and TV shows about addiction, cocaine was promoted as a wonder drug, sold as a cure-all and praised by some of the greatest minds in medical history, including Sigmund Freud and the pioneering surgeon William Halsted. According to historian Dr. Howard Markel, it was even promoted by the likes of Thomas Edison, Queen Victoria, and Pope Leo XIII. It was an explosive debut that would be echoed a century later, when cocaine re-emerged as a different kind of miracle drug, the kind that could let you party all night long with no ill effects and no risk of addiction. "To be a cocaine user in 1979 was to be rich, trendy and fashionable," says Mark Kleiman, a professor of public policy at the University of California, Los Angeles, and co-author of *Drugs and Drug Policy: What Everyone Needs to Know.* People weren't worried about cocaine. It didn't seem to be a problem. Of course, that was a mirage. Each time the enthusiasm was misplaced and the explosion left a wreckage of human lives behind.

The trendy and fashionable allure of the drug was what made me gravitate to cocaine. Yes, as a young person, I did feel the need to fit in, relieve boredom, and seem grown up but the need to fit in among the elite was as important to me as a newborn needing his daily fill of milk. And if there wasn't a chance of addiction, as once thought, what was the problem? I didn't purchase the "powder" at the same run-down duplexes or street vendors where I would buy marijuana. To procure the "wonder drug," one had to be in the know. It was imperative to have a nice job, a nice car, manners, etiquette, charm, and dignity. You had to know somebody, who knew somebody, who knew somebody else who in return could vouch for you as an upstanding, credible, and trusting citizen. If there was the slightest chance that you might be lacking in one or all of those categories, the "connection" would not put his or her good name in jeopardy. It was an unwritten code because this was a special drug for special people.

When you did pass muster and were invited to become a part of the elite culture, there were certain rules of the game that had to be followed at all costs. Since the drugs were usually bought in the suburbs, there was strict emphasis on not bringing attention to oneself. No jalopies, no loud music, no weapons--in essence, no drama. You were expected to engage in meaningful conversation. Current events, achieving world peace, religion, ideology, foreign currency exchange rates, stocks and bonds were some of the topics that I can remember discussing and debating while shoveling grams of the fine white crystal into my septum that would soon become deviated.

The drug seemed to enhance anything that I was involved in at the time. Mundane tasks such as washing the car, vacuuming the floor, cutting the lawn or peeling potatoes all seemed to take on a new light and mystique when high on cocaine. For example, when washing the same car that I had washed over 100 times, I could see colors in the paint that radiated at me; when vacuuming that same carpet that had been in my parents' living room for decades, the patterns of the stitching took on an entirely new shape and appeared as tiny amoeba that would cause my mind to indulge in a biology-infused coma; when cutting that same lawn that I had mowed since grade school, I would imagine photosynthesis taking place and I could see the chlorophyll found in cyanobacteria and the chloroplasts of each individual blade of grass. So if humdrum, tedious, monotonous, and wearisome tasks suddenly sprang to life and became sharper, exciting, fascinating, spirited, and riveting--just imagine how it enhanced things that were already pleasant for me. While intoxicated on the drug and playing basketball I seemed to display moves that I had never even dreamed of while sober, when talking to girls I seemed to display a certain je ne sais quoi when engaging in romantic banter. Denzel Washington, Jim Brown, or even Captain Kirk from the Starship Enterprise who made love to women from Nebulus One to Garadius IV couldn't hold a candle to the rap that I was putting down on the ladies.

Glamorized in songs, movies and the disco scene, "paradise white," one of the many street names for the drug was becoming as popular in the American lexicon as IBM, Kodak and Chrysler. George Clinton assures his audience that "if you just take a toot [of cocaine] and have a beer, we gonna make

it clear"! This became evident to me in Mr. Bianchi's trigo-
nometry class my freshman year at Jacksonville University.
It all started with a midterm test that I was not prepared to
take. Instead of studying the six trigonometric functions sine,
cosine, tangent, secant, cosecant, and cotangent, I was literally out on a tangent partying. The night before that test I
scored some of the purest "snow" available. I partook of the
fine delicacy until the wee hours of the morning. After attempting to get some sleep, I eventually pulled out my text-
book and haphazardly scanned the test material. My mind
seemed to absorb all the information immediately. My brain
was spinning like an EF5 tornado. My brain was a magnet and
the information was steel. Formulas, equations, domains, and
functions were suddenly as clear as the finest Tiffany's crystal.
Jupiter was in Pluto. The stars all aligned. George Clinton was
right, "he HAD made it clear!"

I never got a wink of sleep that night and was eager to
take the test. Cocaine had cast all my fears to the wind. It
had given me the courage of a conquistador, the sharpness
of a finely forged sword, the confidence of a man holding a
royal flush in a game of poker. I was not to be denied. As the
instructor distributed the exam, I somehow felt the effects of
the drug wearing off like a lion springing back to life after being sedated by a researcher's tranquilizer. I quickly excused
myself and hurried to the closest restroom and took another
"hit," like Superman racing through the city to find an unoccupied phone booth to transform from mild-mannered Clark
Kent to "the man of steel." A glance in the mirror, a quick
check of the nose to make sure I inhaled all the evidence, and
I was again stronger than a locomotive and back to leaping

buildings in a single bound.

I made it back to room 127. The room seemed to have grown in size, faces seemed clearer, the light was brighter, I was more confident than a steer in a corral full of cows. The test was placed on the tiny desktops that each student occupied. The paper had the dampness and smell of just being copied on an old AB Dick copier. I picked up my yellow number 2 pencil and got underway. I pondered the answers on only a few of the questions but otherwise zipped through the exam with the greatest of ease. Without checking my work, I turned my test in and strode out of the room with my head held high, sure of myself but not overly ecstatic, like Barry Sanders crossing the goal line and tossing the ball to the official. The results of the test revealed what I had suspected all along--I made an "A" and attributed it all to cocaine, not me. I was just the mechanism used to scribe the actual data on paper, but the true hero was my new best friend, the white lie.

I went the next two semesters trying that same successful formula, and it ended up being instead a prescription for disaster. I was placed on academic probation faster than a bullet fired from 357 Magnum, and eventually kicked out of the university and as a midshipman in the Naval Reserve Officer Training Corps. What I had worked eighteen years to achieve was snorted away in less than a year. I had literally and figuratively blown it. I was hurting on the inside and smiling on the outside. I chalked it up to bad karma and the fix would be easy, I would just enroll at the local junior college and continue own with my studies without missing a beat. It wouldn't be quite as glamorous, but math is math wherever it is being taught, right?

I was dating a young lady named Anita at the time and she wanted to get married. Her mother was a well-respected manager at a very large insurance company, so I did what a good addict would do, I used her. I was able to land an entry-level position with the insurance giant based solely on nepotism. I was to be the future son-in-law of an executive. Although it had a nice ring to it, the most important element of living a life together forever was missing: love. I went to work in corporate America and what I saw excited me. There were 800 employees under one roof and the overwhelming majority were women. I was like a shark trapped in a public swimming pool--this was going to be easy.

My drinking had escalated to epic proportions. Each day after work I was a regular customer through the drive-thru of Jax Liquors off Baymeadows Road that was literally in walking distance of the office. Each night was different but basically the same--I would drink and party until the favors ran out or I passed out. I would then wake up in the morning and drink some more to get me started and on my way. There were times when I would consume as many as four sixteen-ounce malt liquors before going to work at 7 a.m. This led to smoking marijuana at lunch and, when available, snorting cocaine throughout the day. Although I was perceived as a hardworking, well-spoken, and well-meaning young man, the subtle signs of self-destruction were peering through like light through a shade less window. I began to miss days from work; I was moody, unpredictable, and extremely volatile. I was becoming unsure of myself and for the first time in my life, I was blaming others for my misfortunes.

I started listening to an American hip-hop group called

Public Enemy. They are known for politically charged lyrics and criticism of the American media, with an active interest in the frustrations and concerns of the black community. They emphasized that the black man can be just as intelligent as he is strong, that we are not third-world people, we are indeed first-world people; we are the original people of the earth. I ran with this like a bank robber with no car. I was now a college dropout, a confidence man, an addict, and a militant. My plate was full of mess and my life was stalling like a 1979 Ford Pinto in need of an engine.

I worked with several different personalities in corporate America. Some of those coworkers enjoyed the things that I liked; others ran away from them like roaches scattering when the light comes on. One such person was Mr. Lyman T. Johnson, aka Nap. We all called him Nap because he was from Indianapolis by way of Michigan City, Illinois, by way of Chicago. He had made his way to "Good Neighbor Land" via his sister, Yolanda, who worked in the claims department. I was first introduced to Nap in the mailroom where he and I shared a cubicle and sorted mail. He wore a thick black sweater with too many designs on it, the kind that Bill Cosby wore on his hit '80s sitcom *The Cosby Show*. He was a big burly guy with a deep voice that reminded you of the famous actor and orator James Earl Jones, and in speaking with him for just a few minutes; I could deduce that he was wise beyond his years. Although he was about five years younger than me (which seems like a lot when you are in your twenties) we would start a friendship that was genuine, sincere, and no-nonsense.

There were other notables in our department, known as

Administrative Services, which was the branch of the company that made it run smoothly, the engine in the Ferrari, the uranium at the nuclear power plant, the equipment personnel for an NFL football team. Terry Merritt was six years older than me and took on the role as "General" in our inner circle. He was low-key, cerebral, and methodical in his approach to life and I respected and sought out his words of wisdom on many occasions. He was tall and thin with an earring in one ear, and drove a black-on-silver Nissan 280ZX with "T" tops--removable tinted glass Targa tops that gave the driver that "almost convertible feeling." He had a style and persona like no other that I had seen, sporting "parachute pants" and high-top casual boots; he was indeed a maverick in the fashion world.

And just like any faction or clique, there were other components that made it all come together, from the girls in the sorting room to the race-sensitivity-lacking supervisor. I was a functioning addict at this time and I would show glimpses of maturity and career development. I was chosen to represent our unit for some extensive training at a new state-of-the-art facility being built. This was a stand-alone monstrosity that would make our team more efficient and productive to the more than 1,000 agents that we served daily. I flew to Bloomington, IL, corporate headquarters for our company, along with our lead team member. Dale was a good old boy who bled the company's blood and was, in my mind, always out to get me.

I packed all the essentials for the trip: clothes, toothbrush, and pre-rolled marijuana cigarettes neatly inserted in a box of traditional cigarettes. I made sure that my stash was concealed in a sock wrapped around a handkerchief and cleverly insert- ed in the toe section of a size-thirteen Johnston and Murphy loafer. I had become quite the collector of nice wristwatches and had amassed a cache of Seiko and Bulova time pieces. I selected four of my finest and haphazardly tucked them away in one of the side panel of my luggage. We flew out of Jacksonville International Airport on an early-morning flight.

This was my first commercial flight experience, so when the flight attendant asked me if I wanted something to drink, I countered with, "You mean I can have an alcoholic beverage at 8:00 in the morning?"

"Of course, Mr. Preston," was her answer.

I was already 35,000 feet off the ground and getting closer to heaven by the minute. I drank from that moment until land- ing. This also was my first time seeing snow, a Florida boy in the Midwest in February. It was brutal. There was no alco- hol being sold in my hotel, so I quickly trampled through the snow to find a convenience store. I eventually found what I was looking for: alcohol. I made it back to the room to watch the NBA All-Star game and discovered another problem. There were no refrigerators in the small Holiday Inn where we were staying. I looked about the room and then peered out the window--there it was, the answer to my dilemma. I had giant refrigerators formed perfectly by Mother Nature in the middle of the night. I placed my beer in the middle of the snowdrifts and it worked better than any Igloo or Coleman could have ever imagined.

When I finally got down to the business of unpacking, I noticed that someone had rummaged through my belong- ings. I panicked like a diabetic that was unsure of where their next dose of insulin was coming from, like a dialysis patient arriving for treatment only to be told that the center was now closed. I scrambled through the clutter of clothes and toiletries. I noticed that my prized watches were missing, one of which had been given to me by my father, and my heart sank to my stomach. I quickly grabbed the black penny loafer--I could see Abraham's Lincoln head on the shiny copper coin protruding from the slit across the front of the shoe for which they are named. Sweat appeared on my forehead. I thrust my hands down into the crevice where the bullion was so cleverly stashed. I prayed to God that my fix would still be intact. I noticed that the maroon and gray argyle was missing and the kerchief had been removed from its not-so-ominous place. Out the corner of my eye, I noticed that familiar fern-green hue of the clandestinely placed cigarette box. The sweat dissipated from my brow, my nerves were now at ease; part of my watch collection was stolen but I would have the crutch that I was so heavily becoming dependent on, with me in my time of need.

I had temporarily relocated geographically but brought the permanent Richard with me. I drank every time I had the opportunity on that company-sponsored trip and when we returned to the regional office to debrief our team on what we had learned from our experience, Dale rose to his feet, shuffled some papers and announced to a crowded conference of managers, supervisors, technicians, and clerks, "Richard sure can drink!" He was hitting the proverbial nail on the head with his comments and I, being the consummate alcoholic, had blinders on like a champion three-year-old colt running in the famed Kentucky Derby.

Nap and I had developed a friendship that was predicated on mutual respect, trust, and admiration, so the more I increased my usage, I knew this was something that I would not be able to divulge to him. But as we started hanging out more and more, it was becoming difficult to conceal my love of the drug. There were unexplained phone calls that I had to take in private, or visits from guys that were not in our everyday circle of friends, or the times at parties when I would disappear into locked bedrooms with virtual strangers only to re-emerge, recharged, revitalized, revamped, reinvigorated, and readjusted.

As time passed and my usage increased, other parts of my life started to decrease. My work performance was beginning to suffer as an apparent byproduct of long, hard, sometimes sleepless nights. My finances were dwindling, my attention to detail lacking, my love life nonexistent. I remember picking Anita up on a bright, cool Sunday morning to attend 11 a.m. services at her church, Dayspring Baptist Church located on Jefferson Street in Uptown Jacksonville. I was fighting a hardcore hangover this particular morning and needed some help in getting my day started. This is referred to as "biting the hair of the dog that bit you last night" in the twisted mind of a chronic drinker. As she approached the car, her first observation was a sixteen-ounce (tall boy) ice-cold Budweiser beer resting comfortably in the cup holder of the car with beads of fresh condensation dripping slowly into the console of my car and like a segue for an anchorman into their next news story she quietly and without malice or concern stated the words that I will never forget as long as I shall live: "You, my friend, are going to be busting AA's doors down."

I looked deep into her dark brown eyes and without saying a word, gave her a frigid stare and "turned up" the can, wiped the excess from my lips, gave a smug grin, put the car in drive, and continued my journey to her proclamation.

I was first introduced to Alcoholics Anonymous by way of the Employee Assistance Program offered at work. The EAPs are employee benefit programs offered by many employers. They are intended to help employees deal with personal problems that might adversely impact their work performance, health, and well-being. The programs generally include short-term counseling and referral services for employees as well as their household members for issues that may range from concerns about aging parents, work relationship issues, emotional distress, and substance abuse. I was becoming a common face at the nurse's station. I had more frequent flyer miles than Charles Lindbergh. This was another exceptional company benefit at my disposal to abuse.

To call out sick for work, instead of calling my immediate supervisor, the company mandated that you called into the medical department, which was manned by two genuinely concerned registered nurses, Karen and Rita. Karen was a tall, kind, gentle and caring middle- aged lady with a voice as soft as ice cream left in a parked car in July. She never interrogated me when calling in sick or gave me the impression that she had any suspicions of my drinking. Rita, on the other hand, was a thin lady with shorter hair and came off as more of the Columbo of the medical team. When she answered the phone there were more questions as to "Why aren't you coming in" than if Karen had answered the phone with her sweet delicate voice simply replying, "I hope you feel better."

On one particular day after crashing my Stockpicker, a state-of-the-art machine we used in the stockroom to fill the orders for our more than 1000 agents. I had to report to medical for a busted lip that occurred when I slammed the vehicle into a concrete barrier installed to keep workers, not drunks, from accidentally running into shelves that were over 20 feet high. I had consumed countless drinks the night before and close to a six-pack before starting my shift. There was no time to insert five peppermints into my mouth or chew three or four pieces of Wrigley's Spearmint and hope for the best.

The look on Karen's face was incredulous when she saw the condition that I was in at work. She maintained her professionalism and kindness and simply swabbed the blood from my lips applied the antibiotic, and then uttered the words that I did not want to hear: "I am going to let Rita look at you for a second opinion." Rita got close up into my face as if she was going to French kiss me, turned and looked at Karen in utter amazement at my condition, then motioned for me to go lie down. The "sick room" was painted a faint battleship gray and smelled of isopropyl, witch hazel, and antiseptics. On the walls were posters on good nutrition and exercise. There were two twin-sized beds on either side of the room draped in that white crunchy disposable paper that is used in doctor's offices, and which has the consistency somewhere between a brown paper bag and sandpaper.

I climbed onto the one located in the corner farthest from the door and as I lay there looking at the ceiling, I wondered what was I doing to myself--and most importantly, how I was going to stop this runaway train before it ran out of track. I came to a few hours later. I could hear the hushed sounds of the good cop/bad cop discussing the awful situation that they had just experienced. I was excused to leave for the day--next stop Jax Liquors. I was mad at myself, not for the condition that I was in, but for somehow letting the cat out of the bag, because before this episode I was just a regular Joe, an employee with hopes, goals, dreams, and aspirations similar to my counterparts. The following day I was called to medical and given literature on alcoholism and AA for me to read. Karen was almost in tears and Rita had that "Why are we wasting time on this drunk? Fire his behind now!" look on her face.

I was, of course, in denial. To be a good drunk, the prerequisite is to be in denial. If you do not believe that there is a problem and things that never happened in your life are starting to happen and you just happened to be intoxicated during those times, as Jay Foxworthy says in his stand-up comedy routines when he asks oneself to ponder the question after given the answer, "You might just be a redneck" but just remove the word redneck and insert addict. This simplistic but complicated trait can be found in all substance abusers at some point in their life. The Big Book reminds us that "no person likes to think he or she is bodily and mentally different from his fellows." The book of Alcoholic Anonymous (generally known as The Big Book because of the thickness of paper used in the first edition) is a 1939 basic text, describing how to recover from alcoholism, primarily written by one of the founders of AA, Bill W. but with one chapter, "To Employers," written by Henry Parkhurst. According to Wikipedia, it is the originator of the seminal "twelve-step method" widely used to attempt to treat many addictions, from alcoholism and heroin addiction to marijuana addiction, as well as overeating, sex addiction, gambling addiction, with a strong spiritual and social emphasis.

I was somewhat grateful for what the nurses had offered, but I felt that they were jumping the gun with their diagnosis of my having not only having a drinking problem, but any kind of problem. My mind was still intact; I could reason and find solutions to problems better than most. I lived in an ultra-modern luxury apartment complex with all the amenities. I got my hair cut once a week and wore the latest fashions. I had all my teeth, didn't live on skid row, loved my parents, donated to the United Way, and believed in God. I was the opposite of all the stereotypes that I had grown to see in movies and television. My biggest problem was being dumb enough to not conceal my drinking better.

So instead of seeking the help that was so freely offered to me, I chose to drink smarter and fly "under the radar" with my knuckle headedness. No more drinking on the way to work--the absolute cutoff point for partying ended at midnight each night, no liquor on weekdays, always have breath mints at my disposal, this woeful list of "how to be an undercover drunk" was just me being in denial. I did manage to stay out of harm's way and although I wasn't the best that I could be, I thought my work performance was equal to or better than my co-workers. My promotions continued and I was even chosen for the Disaster Relief Team--this team would be on call to assist in catastrophes. While the workers closest to the calamity would mobilize to the stricken area with mobile units, office supplies, tents, power generators, phone lines and data ports, our team would resume their duties in their respective regional office.

On September 16,1988, Hurricane Gilbert ravaged the Gulf Coast and I was called into action. Dale, myself, and another team member were asked to work in Austin's regional office while its relief workers were in the field. And although we were there for humanitarian efforts, my only thoughts were on how to keep my drinking on the "down low." I came up with a plan of action--use more cocaine than alcohol. Cocaine was odorless, colorless, and pretty much tasteless.

As a result of the drug and alcohol abuse, I became stagnant in my position at the company. Instead of rising to the top, like I had done previously in everything associated in my young life, I was now being passed over for promotions; my quarterly reviews consisted of more "needs improvements" than "expectations met." I was constantly being called on the carpet for infractions. I did not care about the company and I sensed that the feeling was mutual. My life was crumbling away like old stale bread in the wind. The two Terrys stuck by me as much as they could without jeopardizing their careers. T. Merritt had been promoted to our data processing department and T. Johnson was being promoted within the administrative services department. The latter Terry would always warn me, but in a joking way so I didn't grasp the sincerity or gravity of the message, "Boy, you'd better leave that stuff alone." What did he know? I was intelligent, strong-minded, strong-willed and most of all a Preston; things like this didn't happen in our family. Anyway, he had never observed me getting high. Stay out of my business, I got this--besides I can quit it all anytime I want to...I just don't want to do it now.

This is just one of the many excuses that people who are addicted to drugs, alcohol, or whatever use to deny we have a problem. By allowing ourselves to believe that we are in complete control and can somehow "manage" our addiction, we are able to remain addicted by sweeping the problem under the rug. Just as it is hard for us to recognize our flaws when it comes to relationships with our spouses or co-workers, it is even harder for us to see what our substance abuse is doing to ourselves and our loved ones. The engagement to Anita ended abruptly. Thank God--love was getting in the way of me getting high, anyway. I wanted to be emancipated from love, responsibility, and anyone who didn't see things my way. Anita ended the relationship without drama or fanfare; there were no tears shed by either of us, no clothes doused with bleach, or calls to human resources to indict me on the extent of my drinking.

Terry Merritt and I planned an excursion to Daytona Beach to getaway and ease my mind. The "World's Most Famous Beach" is located 90 miles southeast of Jacksonville, or about a six-pack away. I had begun the practice of jokingly approximating miles by how many beers you could drink before you got to your destination. I took enough "raw dog" along with me to snort from sun up to sun down and never worry about running out. We had a fabulous time in the sand and surf of the home of NASCAR. Driving up and down the beach and "hollering" at the girls. It was on the return trip back to the "bang 'em" that I realized something was amiss inside my craw. My stomach ached and I was nauseous, but I didn't feel the need to throw up. My head throbbed in pain, but it wasn't excruciating. My appendages were jittery and hard to control. What was wrong with me?

"T" dropped me off at my parents' home, not knowing

how I was feeling because I didn't divulge my symptoms to him--after all, everything I had done to myself that day were self- inflicted wounds. I put my key in the lock, turned the key, and my loving mom met me in the living room and with a mother's intuition, instantly knew that something wasn't right. I asked if I could lie down and of course she obliged and offered to soothe and comfort me in any way that she could.

As she retired to her bedroom, I could hear her telling my father about me. "He's just drunk...I can smell it all the way back here."

My father reassured my mom, "When he sleeps it off he'll be all right."

I was hoping that he was right too, but I had the drinking maturity of someone fifteen years older than me and knew that this was more than a mere hangover. I tried to sleep, but tossed and turned all night like a salad in a washing machine. Finally, in the early hours of the next day, I drove myself to Methodist Hospital about ten minutes away from west 24th street. As I pulled into the parking lot and exited the car, I collapsed like a bridge with no support beams. My legs were like overcooked pasta, and my head disoriented like a pilot flying into the Bermuda Triangle. One of Wackenhut's finest was alert on his post and heard me hit the pavement like a safe being dropped from a second-story window. I awoke to find my parents standing over me, and my mom was crying. I had never seen my dad cry and he would not disappoint on this occasion.

I was suffering from appendicitis and it required prompt surgery to remove it. Left untreated, the organ would eventually burst or perforate, spilling infectious materials into the abdominal cavity and could potentially be fatal. The surgery was a blur to me but an apparent success. My mom was with me as I came to from the anesthesia. I looked into her pretty brown eyes and cried aloud, "I love you more than anything on this earth, Mom," and she responded by saying, "If you really do, for the love of God please tone down your partying... do it for me. I love all my babies, not one more or less than the next, and I would hate to lose any of you."

This was a medical emergency and nothing else; millions of people went through this routine procedure yearly. I minimized the entire situation and did agree to be more cognizant of my drinking, whatever that meant. The surgery required a three-day stint in the hospital. My dad supplied me with a little spending change for the vending machines in the waiting rooms and a *Playboy* magazine. We had never discussed the "birds and the bees" and it seemed like an odd gift, but at the same time it was cool. It was a rite of passage that was never discussed, but implied.

Tom was a co-worker that I had developed a relationship with at work. His dad was a manager in our North Florida division; he shared his father's name and genes, but the similarities pretty much stopped there. His dad was clean-cut, conservative, and mild-mannered--and Tom, well, he was like me: rebellious, cocky, promiscuous, and a lover of bud-smoking. Tom came into my room carrying an '80s version of what today would be called a backpack. It was a modern-day survival pack for the substance-controlled, and he started pulling out "goodies" quicker than a magician pulls a rabbit out of a hat. The kit included several miniature bottles of assorted liquor, JOB rolling papers, beer, a lighter, air freshener--and yes, folks, a bag of high- grade smoke. He rolled a couple of doobies and placed them on my food tray between the small container of chicken broth and the Styrofoam pitcher of ice water. I was placed on a clear liquid diet by my doctor and vodka was clear and fluid, so it fell in the parameters of what I was allowed to have during my recovery from what was then considered major surgery.

T. Merritt was the next person to come see me. When he arrived, he gently pushed the door ajar, poked his head in the door and shouted, "Oy! Oy!" This was a standard reciprocal made up pronoun that Nap, "T," and I referred to one another by as a standard greeting. He entered my small private room that had a 19-inch color Zenith television mounted in the corner of the wall and explained how he had made up some excuse while he would be late to work in order to come visit me. He slid the bulky sky blue vinyl chair that looked like it belonged in an episode of *Nanny and the Professor* and we talked. It turned out to be a very short visit and in retrospect, I believe that he was checking to make sure that he was not going to be an accomplice in the death of a friend that had overdosed. For the next few days my routine was the same: take my vitals, drink my clear liquids, wait on the doctor, asked if I had passed gas yet, go to sleep, watch more boring television, take my vitals, smoke dope in the bathroom.

The most important part of that routine was the "passing gas" question. After this particular surgery in order to be cleared for release, one had to muster up a good strong fart. I was told by the nurse that passing of this foul wind or actually having a bowel movement would be a good sign that the digestive system was in good working order and it was then and only then, a patient was granted a release. I was beginning to become a problem patient--imagine that, with my extracurricular activity and one of the year's biggest pool parties was going down Saturday. I was allowed to eat eggs and bacon Saturday morning and I promptly gave them what they were looking for medically. I was granted my release and somehow hoodwinked the staff into letting me wait in the parking lot for my ride. I looked in the distance and to my surprise--I had forgotten that I drove myself to the hospital—there was my car.

I went through my belongings, found my key, slid in the driver's seat, and almost blacked out from the pain. I had forgotten that I had enough staples in me to sink the Titanic. I steadied myself, wiped the sweat from my brow, and proceeded to the spot to get a dime bag. I would need this later because I had every intention of going to the biggest party of the year. I arrived around 10 p.m. to everyone "shaking what their mama gave them" and plenty of booze. The pain in my belly was excruciating when I walked, talked, or laughed, but I was the man, the tough guy, John Wayne, Clint Eastwood-- these guys would take a bullet and still stammer into the saloon to have a shot of their favorite whiskey, and I was out to prove that I was as brave... or as stupid.

Since I was no longer engaged (not that it had mattered when I was) I started dating ladies from within the office with no sheepishness or penitence whatsoever. They never lasted over a month because after the resume of myself was submitted, the interview was passed, the first date survived, in the end the real Richard would eventually rear his ugly head. Richard the liar, the cheat, the moody guy, the broke guy, the unreliable guy, the hateful guy--I was impulsive as well as compulsive. My tolerance level with alcohol and drugs was now at an all-time high; in other words, a six-pack wasn't doing the trick anymore, a dime bag of weed was for a single usage, and a gram of coke wasn't moving the "high-o-meter" much anymore.

I met a young lady from the Mandarin section of town, which was about 25 miles from where I was living at the time. This proved to be just the buffer I needed to pull off my fraudulent claims of chivalry, grandeur, and maturity to the unsuspecting lass with little or no experience in the sort of debauchery that I was putting down. I wooed her with my lies, promises, and confidence that came to me as naturally as freshly squeezed juice from oranges handpicked from the tree only minutes before drinking it. I took this scheme to an entirely different level and on March 6, 1990 she gave birth to our beautiful daughter Courtney Marie Preston at Memorial Hospital located on University Boulevard on the south side of town.

I, predictably, was not there for the actual birth. I was about two miles north of the hospital, at the Happy Jax Bar. It was a dark, smoky tavern adjacent to a Jax Liquor package store. It was unpretentious, spirited, and cozy and was built around its guests. The jukebox was loud, the lights were dim, and they served freshly popped corn with lots of salt to keep you drinking. It catered to patrons who wanted a drink at any time. There were no teetotalers, no "I can't drink until after six" wussies, and there wasn't a fruity drink with hints of mint or pineapple chunks even available at this watering hole. This was a whiskey on the rocks, bourbon straight, beer-on-tap type of joint...my type of joint.

I bounced from the maternity ward to my offsite waiting room while my daughter's mom was in labor and on the third trip back to Memorial, the scene had shifted to small hospital room on the same floor with now occupied by one more human being, albeit a tiny one. Courtney had black curly matted hair and noticeably long feet. She was as white as an Irishman in winter, yet her ears were the same color as mine. She was a healthy baby with a strong grip as I poked my finger out for her to grab. I noticed a small hospital band around her arm that annoyed me, but not as much as the cast of characters that were in the room and obviously had seen her before me.

Although I had been drinking profusely, I did not appear drunk and I will attribute it to the moment and adrenaline that was pumping through my body. I was as proud as any father could have or should have been. I had a pocketful of celebratory cigars and I passed them around the room like Peyton Manning on any given Sunday. I looked for similarities between the two of us and it did not take long to see the most glaring one of all--just like her father was known to have, she had tiny little beads of sweat on her nose. This was a quirk that had made me the butt of many jokes in my life, and the old wives' tale says that it is a sign that you are mean and bitter. Her mom and I had never been married and I had heard the expression "mother's baby, father's maybe" on an episode of *Sanford and Son*. I peered into her soft brown eyes and looked at her thick lips and saw a reflection of me. I was given a crash course on how to hold her and she responded to my voice, it was a voice she recognized because I read and recited the alphabet, the Pythagorean Theorem, the Gettysburg address, and Albert Einstein's theory of relativity while she was still in the womb. I held her tightly to my chest, and imagined all the possibilities that a child birthed of my loins would bring to this world.

One of my friends introduced me to a revolutionary concept of combining cooked cocaine, or base, or crack in with marijuana and smoking the two as a combination. I had heard all of the harmful aspects of smoking the stuff, including how it affects brain chemistry of the user, and after just one try the user is usually hooked. That was intriguing to me and I was going to dispel that rumor and prove them all wrong. Once again, they were describing the less- advantaged, the poor, the uneducated--not me. The first time he offered me a juiced joint, I was in love. It gave the weed a sweet, smooth taste and the high was intense but mellowed by the THC in the weed. I became quite the expert on rolling a geek joint, as it became to be known in my circle. The key to a good blended joint was to roughly crush the crack up first; I would then blend the two ingredients together and roll the joint. Then I would take a disposable lighter and gently singe the sides of the joint until the dope caramelized inside and gave the joint a brownish hue on the outside that resembled the spots on a Jersey cow. Light that up and like Jackie Gleason used to say on *The Honeymooners*, "To the moon, Alice--to the moon." This was not a cheap pastime that I had ventured into; initially I was spending $40 to $60 a day to get high, add another $10 to $20 in drinking and it was becoming quite expensive, but it was now taking priority over rent, insurance, utilities, and in a lot of instances, food. I soon had more money going out than coming in and it didn't take a Wall Street wizard to realize this couldn't last long. I was now staying up to wee hours of the morning and traveling back and forth across that same toll bridge that I was so familiar with from my days of high school. I vividly remember on one of my binges, the toll taker had seen my car so many times on this particular night/morning that she said, "It's you again"! To illustrate the magnitude of what she observed, I have to tell you that during those years the bridge had an estimated crossing of 30-40 thousand cars on a given day. Eviction was on the horizon and two months later. Done deal.

I eventually moved in with Courtney and her mother and experienced all the things that a normal father might expect to see, her first steps, her first words, her first teeth—yes, I was privy to all of the wonders of being a new father, but my drinking and drug use were escalating. I was a functional addict at the time and barely living up to my financial, spiritual, and emotional obligations. The crack craze had turned the drug culture inside out. Everything that I wrote about the subculture of powdered cocaine earlier in the book was just the opposite now. Rock could be sold in smaller quantities, to more people, at a bigger profit. It was cheap, simple to produce, easy to use, and highly profitable for dealers. So, instead of purchasing from a dealer in the suburbs who drove a BMW automobile, you were now purchasing your fix on a street corner from little "Jitterbug," whose only means of transportation is a BMX mountain bike that he stole from the corner store. Everyone was in on the action--there were reports of grandmothers, postal workers, policemen, politicians, and preachers arrested for selling arguably the most highly addictive substance known to man. I had conquered Everest, landed on the moon, and found a cure for cancer. I had gone from the frying pan to the fire!

CHAPTER 5
When Keeping It Real Goes....

My final day working for the insurance company came on a Tuesday. I started the morning like most other days, but little did I know that this day would symbolically mark the days that lay ahead for me. I drank a few beers, smoked a joint, listened to some music, and traveled the short distance to the office. I chewed on a couple pieces of watermelon Bubblicious gum like a camel chewing on his cud to mask the smell of the fermented hops that I had for breakfast. A few hours into my shift, I was summoned to the Executive Conference room, which was located at the front of the building and in proximity to the human resources department. I turned the brass handle of the walnut-colored door and entered. I immediately knew why I was there and what was about to transpire.

The vice-president of personnel, the manager of administrative services, and my immediate supervisor were all sitting at the huge rectangular-shaped table. They were all clad in an array of ugly sports jackets that did not match the shirt and tie ensemble that they were wearing. It was cold and the room smelled of nothing, like it had never been used before. As I sat down, the first thing that came into my mind was *How am I going to support my newborn daughter?* and the second was *How am I going to afford to get high?* The top brass spelled out my inadequacies, failure to meets, and unsatisfactory performance like they were the adults on *Sesame Street* reading to a child. Each took their turn solemnly, professionally, and calmly tearing me down--or in this case, trying to tear me up-- but I was not mature enough in life to understand.

A few moments later the head of security knocked on the door in rapid succession like a kid rapping on the door of the neighborhood's secret hideout. He came through the doorway with an old copier paper box with the words MAC papers written on the side, filled with my personal items. With a quick glance, I could see my personal belongings spilling over like lava from a volcano. My awards, ribbons, beer mug with my name inscribed on it, newspaper articles...and I could see on the very top was the picture of my newborn daughter that I cherished and kept in my station. Whoever packed my belongings seemed to have staged it, rightfully so, as a meaningful mnemonic of how I was starting out parenthood on a note as sour as a box of Warheads candy.

I had now shifted my attention on that one supposed act of disrespect rather than how my actions had caused me to lose my career despite all the warning signs, missed opportunities, and all the people that I had hurt along the way. I was in complete denial. After signing all the necessary forms, Jan, the same young lady who had done my onboarding six years ago to the date, in a strange twist of fate, was now putting the final stamp on a career cut way too short by the abuse of alcohol and drugs. After wishing me well in life, she handed me four sealed envelopes with the company's return address printed in the upper left-hand corner. As I was escorted out of the building, in the distance I could see two golf carts with the yellow flashing lights on the roof like Department of Transportation trucks parked in the median of Interstate 95 flanked on either side of my car. The guards held huge radios and every few seconds they would come to life with a loud crackle and someone on the other end asking for an update. This was quickly turning from a covert operation to a full-blown public spectacle.

It was lunch time and the smokers were outside enjoying their post-dining smoke. I had parked in front of the cafeteria and as the diners were enjoying their liver and onions and shepherd's pie, just on the other side of the thick tinted glass, was the show. I opened the door to my Nissan 280ZX and started the engine as Public Enemy's *Fear of a Black Planet* sprang to life at an intense volume. I removed my T-tops, lifted the hatchback, and tried to make this crushing moment go as smoothly as possible. I put the box of belongings in the back and started to fumble through my personal effects. I was approached by Deputy Fife and encouraged to step up the pace. I am sure that I had some not-so-kind words for him--after all, I had nothing to lose now.

I opened each one of the sealed envelopes that had been given me. To my relief, the contents were different documents with more legal jargon than a lease-to-own contract, but each letter had a check made out to me. They were labeled final check, severance check, 401K, and Christmas club check.

And in a strange twist of fate, in my morbid mind, Christmas had just arrived. I hopped into the beige bucket seats of my black sports car, shifted into first gear, redlined the RPMs, and dumped the clutch. The squeal of the Goodyear eagle GT's startled everyone as I fishtailed the backend in the direction of one of the golf carts leaving a trail of white smoke from burning rubber like a Dragster at the Gator Nationals. I merged onto Baymeadows Way and in minutes I was in the parking lot of my local bank cashing in all that I had in life. For the next few weeks I pretended to go to work like you see in the movies, but instead of going to the park and feeding the pigeons, I was going to the package store and dope holes to feed a hunger for something much more than peanuts and popcorn.

Courtney's mom was very naïve and I played her like Ray Charles plays a piano. My manipulation, scheming, and lying skills had graduated from kindergarten and were now in graduate school. I eventually told her that I would never be going back to State Farm. I can't remember which excuse I finally agreed upon for the exodus, but one thing I am sure of is that it was not the truth. I ran through those final checks like Usain Bolt stretching for the finish line tape in the 2008 Beijing Olympics. Although my income and net worth decreased, my drinking increased tenfold in the coming months. I can't attribute the rise in consumption to depression, despair, or desolation from being unemployed--I just loved alcohol, the smell, the effects, the taste.

I started getting creative in my ways to obtain my fix. One of the easiest ways was to write checks at the local supermarkets. The policy for most of the chains allowed for a customer to write a check for groceries, and if needed the guest could request cash back over and beyond the final tally. It was the precursor to swiping a debit card, entering your PIN and selecting cash back. I would buy nice cuts of meat, seafood, baby formula, and beer only to write a check that had no money in the account, receive cash back, and go buy my dope du jour. As each chain caught up with me, which took weeks and sometimes months, I would move to another unsuspecting marketplace and start the con all over again.

On a brisk morning in November, I was asked to pick up few things for Courtney at our neighborhood grocer's. I parked in front of the store. I was going to make a mad dash in, grab a few things, then dart out. As I checked out I noticed a police cruiser behind my car. It didn't alarm me because he was there only for a brief moment, but then I noticed he pulled his car into the stream of law-abiding shoppers that actually parked in the parking lot. He crept at a snail's pace and strategically placed his car in a position that was somewhat stealthy and perpendicular to my car. All of my attention was now on the scene that was unfolding in front of my very eyes. I used money that was given to me by Courtney's mother for this transaction, so what was the problem?

As I left the store, I contemplated leaving the car, but I tried to fool myself into believing that he was not there for me. I put my packages into the passenger's side of the car and slowly walked to the driver's door, all the time seeing that cop car stalking me like a prize fighter sizes up his opponent before the knockout. Out of the corner of my eye I could see the cruiser inch forward, ready to pounce on me like a lion on his prey. I eased away from the curb and before I could look into my rearview mirror his red and blue bubble gum machines came to life. I pulled over in one of the spaces that I should have been in the first place and he approached my car and asked for standard license and registration. I produced both, and being a much ballyhooed fan of the 1970s police action thrillers *Dragnet* and *Adam-12*, I asked the reason for my detention.

He was a tall cop with a clean-shaven baby face and dark-tinted sunglasses. He spoke with a heavy Southern accent in a deep voice that didn't seem like it was made for his body. He politely told me that there were outstanding warrants for my arrest and that although he'd rather be out catching bad guys, he had no alternative but to take me to jail. He placed me in handcuffs and gently put me in the back seat of his car, which smelled of cheap aftershave lotion. I was amazed at the configuration of the inside of the vehicle. It was a cross between a Winston Cup series car and a family car. The radio and computer system were a far cry from the little two-knob Motorola that was a fixture in Joe Friday's 1966 Ford Fairlane. The safety cage in the car that separated the good guy from the bad guy (or vice versa, according to what perspective you are viewing it from) had a sliding partition on it for easier communication between you and your driver taking you to your express getaway. I could hear first-hand accounts of robberies, domestic situations, burglaries, and traffic stops being broadcast over the sophisticated two-way radio network. The car was equipped with rear speakers and he had it tuned into an unfamiliar station that was playing a familiar song, "It's a Beautiful Morning" by the Rascals.

I tapped on the cage to ask a few questions about the

process. He lowered the volume on the music and graciously answered my questions, being careful not to promise anything. He asked a couple of personal questions about me because he was taken aback by my proficiency with and mastery of the English language, obviously something he was not accustomed to coming from someone who was sitting in the back of his car. For lack of a better analogy, he gave me the old "What is a guy like you doing in a place like this?" sentiment. I took it as a compliment, sat back in my seat, and wished for this to be over as soon as possible as he now sang aloud, "It's a Beautiful Morning" in his cross between a Mississippi and Alabama drawl.

He merged onto Beach Boulevard and headed over the Harts Bridge, the same bridge that used to take me home from Sandalwood High, but this time it was so very different as he took the downtown exit instead of the 20th Street Expressway as we did back then. As we arrived at The John E. Goode Pre-Trial-Detention Facility, our final destination, my stomach muscles began to tighten. This was a new facility located on the outer banks of downtown next to the Maxwell House Coffee Plant and literally a stone's throw away from the St. Johns River.

My driver pulled to the rear of the facility and spoke some magic words into a voice box similar to the ones used for ordering a Whopper or a Big Mac at your local neighborhood eatery. The garage-door-type gate, equivalent to several of the standard variety, started to shake and hum as it began its ascent. Just as it cleared the roof of the cruiser, the officer pulled into a cavernous underground world of mystery, intrigue. and anxiety. The electronic door slid open to accept me into my new home, and my guide wished me well as he disappeared into a different entrance. That same door clanged shut behind me with a loud thud. The welcoming committee put on rubber gloves and started frisking me. They made me take off my shoes as they searched in my mouth, ears, and the bottoms of my feet. What? I was given—no, thrown--a brown paper bag like the ones found in any grocery store to put my clothes in. They confiscated my belt, wallet, and what little bit of money that was in my possession. They traded my two-toned silver and gold Seiko with a black alligator band for an Egyptian blue plastic armband that was crudely measured for fit by placing it around my wrist to approximate my size. Next the officer used a black Sharpie to inscribe my entire name and booking number, which was a ten-digit number that began with the last two digits of the current year. The bracelet was then riveted to my arm with a tool that resembled a large pair of pliers. I was asked my size and again thrown another brown with a jungle green uniform inside that is best described as scrubs with no character. The bag also contained a pair of boxer shorts with the letters "XL" written on the lower thigh area. They came standard with skid marks, a slight rip, and threads hanging from the seams. A pair of white crew socks completed the outfit.

I had barely convinced myself to put those used drawers on before my name was being shouted, "PRESTON!!"

I quickly hurried to the window thinking, *the sooner I get through this, the better*. I was now at the property window. At this station, all of your property and money is cataloged in front of you to protect your interest. After counting my few dollars and some change, a black leather belt, my watch, wallet and a 14-karat gold rope bracelet I signed a small rectangular piece of yellow paper that was filled out in triplicate. He separated the canary stationery that had the Jacksonville Sherriff Office's shield printed on the itemized document. I was given a copy and the officer motioned for me to sit in the hallway on the stainless steel bench. The shiny slab was as cold as an enthusiastic New England audience. The walls were painted a drab Columbia blue and the doors to the holding cells were a battleship grey.

I looked around my surroundings and thought, *what a mess I am making of my once-wonderful life*. I thought about my daughter, my mom and dad, Mama Dora, Grand mama Ruby, my brothers, my dignity, my future. The officers waited for the benches to fill before we were ordered to stand and line up against the wall. A female officer approached us as she donned a pair of rubber gloves and motioned for us to face the wall as she instituted another search, with this one being a little more invasive as she checked the rims of my, for lack of a better word, trousers. She looked into my ears, rubbed my privates, and looked into my mouth with a flashlight. She had me take off my shoes as she removed the insoles and banged the left and the right shoe together as if she was playing the cymbals for the New York Philharmonic Orchestra led by Leonard Bernstein. After the crescendo, she tossed them on the ground and moved on to the next contestant.

Once everyone was "shaken down," we were told to follow her and stay on the red line as we walked to the next station. The red line was a series of crimson-colored tiles that had been installed amongst the off-white but high-gloss tile that covered the rest of the floor. The trail twisted and snaked around the cavernous place like the Yellow Brick Road in *The Wizard of Oz*. The path to the inevitable ended and we were hurried through a double door with the words Central Booking stenciled overhead. Next stop was the fingerprinting room, as my entire hand was rolled in jet-black ink with a roller like a painter uses to cover large areas in a short amount of time, and each digit copied onto a red and white 8 ½ by 11 card with spaces for all five fingers of my left and right hands. The palm print was also required to complete the set. The friction ridges left by each one of my digits on the card were quite fascinating to see, but as I glanced at the officer's watch it was now past noon and I was getting nowhere fast. Both of my hands were covered in ink and looked like I had just changed a transmission on a 1969 Ford.

I asked where I could wash my hands and as he was re-peating the same procedure on the next lucky contestant, he motioned to a sink in the back corner of the room. I turned the knob on the faucet but nothing came out. He motioned with a nod of his head to a strategically placed pump of waterless hand cleaner, the kind you see in mechanics' garages and you wonder to yourself, *just how good does this stuff work?* It doesn't.

We were lined up once again outside of this station and given strict orders to pipe down. I was not prepared for what was next in this procedure that was turning into a life's work. Several officers, perhaps five, had desks with small partitions side by side in a spacious area of this particular part of the jail. Each had their own phone, computer, pencil sharpener, stationery, staplers, and drink of choice to sip, and a huge Xerox to share, but there were no pictures of family, no cute coloring masterpieces from little Johnny and Mary, no college or high school memorabilia--just processing stuff. Crossways from that area was what I can only describe as a nightmare in real life. These were holding cells the size of a living room in a 2000-square-foot house, filled to the brim with human-ity...and some of them didn't seem human. There were old and young, black and white, gay and straight, homed and homeless.

When he opened the door to corral us in, the stench was sickening. They had two benches and eight phones for over seventy-five prisoners. Some were sleeping on the floor with rolls of toilet tissue masquerading as pillows. The one toilet was at the rear of the confines with 100 percent exposure for all the world to see, inmates and officers alike. The tem-perature in this hell hole was well below 50 degrees, only to make a nasty situation an uncomfortable situation. Some guys had wriggled their arms out of the sleeves of their uniforms and concealed them under the green uniforms that we all had on. Some nestled their hands in their pants as they caressed their scrotums in an attempt to stay warm. The noise inside the holding cell was deafening as each person discussed their case, sought out bail bond agencies, or cursed at family mem-bers on the receiving end of phone calls. I definitely was not in Kansas anymore, Toto.

Some of my mates looked like me, some looked like the dope dealers that I had come to be so familiar with, others looked like dads, husbands, uncles, and even grandfathers. Many smelled of alcohol, some smelled of urine. There were the articulate, the illiterate, the blind, crippled, and the crazy--but we all had one thing in common at this magical moment in time: we had all lost our freedom.

The guys weren't as tough and nasty as portrayed in Hollywood. The inmates represented a microcosm of society. A UPS driver caught up in a prostitute sting, a "grilled up" drug dealer in for the sale of narcotics, a user in for possession, guys who had violated probation, and scores of domestic cases were discussed as "jailhouse lawyers" offered their services pro bono. The officers would come to the door every few hours with a handful of papers and extract about ten inmates at a time to be processed. Six hours had elapsed since I had been pulled over and I was beginning to get hungry. As I waited patiently but anxiously for my name to be called just to get a break from the loud racket, horrible smells, and redundant conversation, the guards announced that anyone who came in before 12:00 was going to be served lunch shortly.

That shortly happened about an hour later as two trustees wheeled a tan oversized Rubbermaid cart down the hall and stopped in front of the door. The guard had several oversized keys dangling from his patent-leather gun belt that carried no gun but had handcuffs and a can of pepper spray where the gun should have been. He fumbled through the massive keys without looking and nonchalantly selected the correct one to insert into the gigantic tumbler. He pulled the huge door open and motioned for the trustees to wheel the cart in that direction. The carts were full of brown bag lunches like the ones my mom had made countless times for me when I was a child. The officer grabbed four or maybe five at a time and tossed them into the cell like zookeepers tossing treats to the animals. And just like the animals in those cages at the zoo, the inmates sprang to life and converged on those bags like lions being fed raw bloody beef.

I didn't get one on the first round, but I was extremely hungry and I had made up in my mind that when the next wave of morsels was tossed, come hell or high water, I was going to eat. I trampled over one of the smaller inmates like a reveler trampling one of his buddies in Pompeii during the running of the bulls. I cowered in the back of the disgusting room and found a spot on the floor that was not as disgusting as the rest. The bag had a slight rip on the side from me tearing it away from one of my comrades. I unfolded the top and gazed in to my lunch. A blemished orange, an elementary school size carton of 2% milk, a Little Debbie's oatmeal snack cake, and a peanut butter and jelly on white stale bread was the blue plate special. I had read and heard all of my life on just how good the food in jail was with pork chops, steaks, and other fine cuts of meat being served up more than tennis balls at Wimbledon. Maybe they were just holding out until I am processed and then I could dine in the cafeteria.

I couldn't remember my last "choke" sandwich, as we used to call them as kids, but this one ranked up in the top ten best sandwiches since I was so hungry. I finished my meal and threw the brown paper bag, packaging from the cookie, orange rinds, and emptied milk carton on the floor since there was no garbage receptacle and that was what everyone else did, so when in Rome. The overweight officer with one gold chevron stitched on the right sleeve of his light-blue uniform opened up the door to the pig sty that I was in, he had a stack of papers in his hand and barked in a loud and obnoxious voice for everyone to shut up and listen for their names to be called. After calling out several surnames, he bellowed,

"PREESTONE"--close enough for me, and I did not correct him on the pronunciation. I had now been there for over eight hours and still hadn't been officially admitted into the system.

I sat at the officer's desk when she called my name. She was a thin black lady in her late twenties who was quite attractive. She had on too much makeup and smelled like she had just taken a bath in a tub full of Jean Naté. I turned up the charm like the thermostat on a freezing morning in Florida and she looked through me like I was a plate glass window. She informed me of my charges and what it would take for me to bond out. I had thirteen counts of passing worthless checks and defrauding a merchant. It was then I realized that all those checks that I had written to Winn Dixie, Publix, and Food Lion were now hanging over my head like the Sword of Damocles. Each count had a $500 bond and I would be seeing a judge at 9:00 the next morning. She coldly motioned for me to stand and get in line with the gentlemen that had gone before me.

The line was to go back into the disgusting holding cell that now after lunch resembled pictures from Hurricane Dora in 1964. I dreaded going back into that place like a vegetarian invited to a Brazilian Steakhouse. Once the door was open, I rushed in and lay on one of the cold steel benches that had over the years collected the nastiest graffiti that I had ever read. I tried to take a nap to expedite this hell on earth that I was experiencing but it was so loud, stinky, and uncomfortable that sleep was not in the cards. After another hour or so the same officer called out my name only to mispronounce it differently than the previous time, and once again it was cool.

It was now time to see the nurse. The nurse was a thin white lady with a psychedelic- colored jacket covering her scrubs, which were gold in color. She had cat's-eye glasses with some sort of fake jewels on each corner that hang around her neck held there by a silver chain. She had a raspy low-pitched voice like Lucille Ball and smelled of Benson and Hedges menthol 100's. She weighed me and measured my height as an old chrome-plated stethoscope hung from her neck. She motioned for me to have a seat in front of her desk and was unmoved by my politeness and respect. Like a Marine with an M-16, she fired off questions in rapid succession, seemingly jotting down answers before I actually responded, with the last question being, "Do you feel like hurting yourself today?"

She instructed me to go sit on the bench in the hallway to wait for further instructions. It was colder than Vermont in January as I waited for my next instructions. I looked around in disgust as I got a glimpse of one of the passing officer's watch. It had been approximately nine hours since I had pulled over at my neighborhood grocer's, and I was no closer to going home than when I started this trek through our famed justice system. My name was called and about six of us were corralled into yet another holding cell about the size of a standard bathroom. There was another long wait in here as I was informed by some past guests of the facility that it was now shift change for the officers. The Isley Brothers song "Hurry Up and Wait" played over and over again in my head. Due to the cold temperature in the cell, my metabolism had slowed like live blue crabs when you put them in the freezer.

When this door sprang to life after what seemed like an eternity, we were called out individually by a new crew of "screws." The only difference was the faces--the attitudes and dispositions remained the same. As each name was called, we were issued a small plastic baggie with a small bar of soap, a toothbrush, comb, and disposable razor and instructed back out into the hallway where two trustees were standing by a large canvas cart with bed rolls stacked to the top. The bed rolls were an ugly chocolate brown, like the ones Clint Eastwood would unfold in the heart of desert country in some of his famous Westerns. They were made of wool and I immediately began to itch just from looking at them. As each of us grabbed a roll, we were issued a housing assignment. We compared assignments and wondered why they differed so vastly. Some of us were going to the second floor, some to the first--but we did notice that if you were charged with a felonious act, those folks were off to the fifth floor and nobody was going home...at least not at this moment.

We all headed off in the direction that we were told and ended up at the elevator. At first glance it looks like your standard Otis or Miami garden-variety type of lift, but upon closer inspection I could not locate the standard buttons to ask whether I would like to go up or down. Also, there was no indicator as to what floor your chariot was on, although you could hear the loud rumbling sounds of the powered dumbwaiter. As I pivoted my body 180 degrees, to my astonishment I could see an officer surrounded by glass in a modular control booth with a control panel that resembled the bridge on the Starship Enterprise, yelling at us to step back. In seconds our ride had arrived. "Floors 2 through 6," he hollered. We all entered the stainless-steel monstrosity that was actually a modified Otis elevator. There were no lights, no dings and dongs as we stopped at each level; the buttons were really no buttons at all, but silver plates where the selections should have been, and at each stop the ever-present guard in the control booth lay in wait.

I disembarked on the fourth floor whether I wanted to or not, and handed my cell assignment to the guard. He motioned for me to head to the east section of the floor. He pushed some buttons and a huge blue door sprang to life and began to slide to the right. The door read 4 East and the glass on the door was at least four inches thick. There was a deafening silence as I stepped over the threshold and began walking. The door started to slide behind me and closed with a loud thud like the sound of a manhole cover being dropped off of a two-story building. I was now in a cold, dimly lit hallway with high glossed vinyl floors that looked like they were buffed every day. It reminded me of the long stretch that the characters in *The Wizard of Oz* had to walk before seeing the Almighty One. I could see in the distance that I would be approaching another control booth.

I came to another automatic cell door that again sprang to life when I approached and quickly closed as I stepped through its plane. The atmosphere, if not already bad enough, was wicked and sinister. I could see inmates now. It had been only minutes, but it seemed like much longer since the last time I had seen human beings. In one glance, I saw a microcosm of society locked in what I would get to know as a pod. White, Black, Asian, Latino, homosexual, tall, short, fat, bald, old, young, athletic, skinny...some were in wheelchairs, some missing eyes, arms, or legs. At this security checkpoint, the officer came down from his perch inside the electronically secured tower and met me at a battleship-grey steel door that buzzed, then suddenly opened as he pushed it ajar. He was careful not to let it close behind him as he positioned his body between the door and the jamb. He asked for my cell assignment, which was written on my arrest docket paperwork. He looked over my credentials, asked to see my state- issued armband, and gave me back the paperwork. He made his way back up a small set of stairs in the master control room as the door clanged shut behind him.

I was invited into series of dormitories that all had glass walls and no bars; the officer was now speaking to me through an intercom system. The walls of each housing unit were clearly marked in huge black letters as I looked for my address. There it was, 2 East. As I peered into the transparent walls of the dorm, I could see all types of "activities" taking place. There were guys lifting homemade weights ingeniously constructed out of a mop handle with two Hefty bags full of water on each side. A spades game was hot and heavy as guys slammed cards down on the smooth stainless-steel tables, making a smacking sound that sounded like a whip being cracked in the air as each player yelled out obscenities and boastful phrases like "You don't want none of this," or "ain't no fun when the rabbit got the gun" or predicting the outcome and yelling "Who's next?" while the game was still being played. Some of my fellow mates walked laps around the small dorm that housed what seemed like 500 guys, but was probably more like 50. There was a long line waiting to use the telephones that were bolted to the walls, because only two of the four phones in the dorm actually worked.

All of a sudden the crackle of the intercom could barely be heard as the officer barked out a command, "stand back" he yelled through the small Motorola system and the door began to glide open slowly like a freight train pulling into the station. The noise increased to the power of ten, the smells that permeated through the air were unrecognizable, the temperature got even colder and I reasoned with myself, *I am in jail but I am better than the rest of these guys, they need to be in jail and I am just passing through on a humbug tip.* I was barraged by a number of my cohorts asking questions like "What are you in for?" "Are you going to bond out?" and the number question was "Are you going to eat that tray when it comes?" I answered a few of them in a firm and decisive way because as I had heard, to be meek and frail in here was not a good thing. I climbed the stairs to the upper level where my cell was located. I was hungry, weary, and really quite bewildered about how I had gotten caught up in this predicament.

I walked into my assigned cell and unfolded my bed roll onto the available bunk in the small two-man quarters. There were two slabs of steel aligned in an "L" shape, with one being along the side wall and the other placed horizontally against the back wall. There a small writing table made of solid steel and a steel toilet and sink combination that sat no more than six inches from the head of the bed. I started to unfold my bed roll to reveal its contents. There was a washcloth, a sheet, and a pillowcase--yet there was no pillow in the room. My cellmate suddenly appeared and introduced himself. I can't remember his name, but he was a tall black dude with short nappy hair and skin the color of dark chocolate. He was wearing his state-issued green pants with the words Jacksonville Sherriff's Office tattooed down the right pant leg. He wasn't wearing a shirt and was sweating like he had just finished running from the police. He told me what he was accused of and how he was falsely accused, set up, and framed. After listening to what seemed like hundreds of phone calls in the holding cells, this seemed to be the common sentiment in central lockup--no one was guilty.

I explained why I was arrested and my "bunkie" instantly became astute of the law, a Matlock with a teardrop engraved under his right eye. I knew that I was guilty of the charges brought against me by the State of Florida and I just wanted to stand before a judge and beg for mercy to be freed from this invading, humiliating place. I excused myself and tried to get some sleep, but I kept replaying my life in my mind. I thought of happier times, which was every single minute that was not spent in this place. How did James and Mary's boy get off the path of righteousness and find the dark, cold, and lonely street of crookedness and dishonesty? I had surely disgraced the Preston name, reputation, and honor, but how did I get here so quickly? I thought of my cute young daughter and the way she smelled after taking a bath in the sink. I thought of everything pleasant to try to filter out the utter filth, nastiness, and shame that were before me.

The guys intuitively began to muster around the huge door that I had entered through only minutes ago. The intercom came to life without warning and the officer screamed "chow time." This sparked a frenzy of movement like chickens when Old Farmer Brown steps into their coop and flings some of his best feed around. Then I glanced over the cold steel railing and I could see two trustees and the officer arriving at the door with a large stainless-steel cart that resembled a mid-sized refrigerator on wheels. Then almost in unison the guys in the dorms started shouting what the officer on the intercom had bellowed just minutes before: "Chow time! Chow time!" The spectacle caught my eye and I gazed in amazement at the sheer crass, brutish, subhuman, animalistic event that was happening right before my very eyes. The officer gave the nod to the officer's in the control room to "roll" the door and the huge door opened like door number two on *Let's Make a Deal*. I was famished but I stayed to the rear of the quickly forming single-file line to figure out the protocol for jailhouse dining before I did something that I might regret.

The unlikely team of officer and trustees worked in tandem like tenured assembly line workers. The officer checked each inmate's armband as he made a quick search for your name on his computer generated roster as one trustee handed out a cup of tea and the other shoved a thick mud-colored tray into your mitt. Some of the guys danced a jig as they received the rations, while others were not as grateful complaining that someone had "shaken the spoon" on them, a slang phrase that simply meant that the received portion was insufficient. Some went and put their meal on one of the many steel tables that looked like small picnic tables, but instead of being made out of cedar or pine, these were forged out of the same material that is used in ship construction and bolted to the floor with bolts and screws large enough choke an elephant. The fellows began to barter and trade items off their trays at a loud and furious clip that would have certainly gotten you expelled from elementary school. The main dish was baked chicken, mashed potatoes, some sort of green leafy vegetable, and a Little Debbie's Oatmeal raisin snack cake. I patiently awaited my turn for the feast as the line began to shrink. Knowing that

I was the new kid on the block, the officer seemed to inspect my Rolex, which is jailhouse jargon for an armband, with a little more care. Table capacity was four so I panned the room for an opening; I found a spot and surveyed the grub set forth before me. I reached for my salt and pepper packet to sprinkle but it had been haphazardly placed in the same slot as my vegetables that were swimming in a sea of brine.

I guess my tablemates could see that I was somewhat hesitant about diving into my vittles and in harmony, like a barbershop quartet, began asking me "Are you going to eat this, or you going to eat that, can I have your chicken?" Before I could take a bite of anything, some guys were already finished with the less-than-filling meal. I sampled the vegetables first. The greens had no taste and the potatoes were palatable, but did not taste like any spud that I had ever eaten before. The chicken was bland, unseasoned and undercooked; I took a few nibbles and decided I had my fill of the less-than-sumptuous meal. The guys realized what was happening and was moving in for the kill. They resembled vultures waiting for their prey to breathe a final breath. I could hear guys screaming from the other side of the day room, "Hey man, if you aren't going to eat that, I'll take care of it for you," and yet others used a more implied tactic by saying things like "Hey man, you don't want that mess" and yet others used a more scholarly and positive approach by exclaiming, "Brother man, you gonna be out of here tomorrow, hook a brother up."

I decided it was not in my best interest to choose one over the other, so I grabbed my cake, which is referred to as a "sweetie gold" in the jailhouse vernacular, and headed to my cell. Unbeknownst to me, I was on the verge of inciting a riot because those boys fought over those unappetizing morsels longer than most Mike Tyson fights had lasted. I had taken solace in the fact that my peers were confident that I was going to be sprung in the morning after seeing the judge, so I decided to retire early. The noise was deafening as I lay in my bunk. Some guys were banging on the tables and singing, while others screamed obscenities at the guards through panes of double-sided Plexiglas, to no avail. Dominoes were being slammed on the thick steel tables with enough force to register seismic activity on the Richter scale. Trivial debates such as who was the best NBA center ever, Daryl Dawkins or Wilt Chamberlain, who made the best hamburger, McDonalds or Burger King, who was finer Maryann or Ginger from the old show *Gilligan's Island* escalated into heated arguments that nearly turned into full-blown fisticuffs. I wanted to wake up from this nightmare and paradoxically, the only way to do that was to fall asleep. I had been promised to see a judge at 9:00 the next day who would determine my fate and it could not come soon enough. I had not said a prayer since those old days at Henry Gordon, but that streak was broken as I asked the Lord to get me out of this mess, and I even promised Him that if He did, I would give up the drinking and the drugs.

"Chow time!" was the alarm that woke me up the next morning. I rubbed my eyes, looked around and although I had just awakened, the nightmare continued. My "celly" immediately began asking me if I was going to eat this or could he have that off of my breakfast tray. There was no good morning or how did you sleep exchange offered to butter me up; instead he advised me that I had no time to wash my face or brush my teeth and could he have my orange juice. In the environment it was a must to have a calm exterior, but on the inside I was disheveled, like a 1000-piece jigsaw puzzle that had been in a paint shaker. I wanted to cry, I needed a hug, I wanted my mama!

I made it downstairs just before the last tray was passed out. The guard gave me some not-so-kind words for him having to wait an extra ten seconds to serve me what looked like something I had regurgitated on a bad Saturday night. I would soon be educated that this was one of the more coveted meals on the corrections cuisine carousel. The formal name of the dish was chipped beef on toast, but in jail jargon is was aptly named "stuff on a shingle." Its nickname comes from its resemblance and texture to solid waste produced by humans and/or animals. Some of the guys just called it "shank," which, I guess was a contraction of two words that I do not know. It was served alongside a dab of oatmeal that looked like Thelma from the 1970s sitcom *Good Times* had cooked it. A small carton of 2% milk and orange juice were the beverages of choice. The loud bartering and trading that went on with dinner was back in full swing as guys scratched their private parts, rubbed cold from their eye sockets, and grumbled about their conditions.

I swilled my drinks, called my roommate and pushed my tray in his direction, and received one of the most appreciative smiles that I had ever seen, like a man marooned on a desert island being rescued after years of giving up hope. I went over to the PA system located in front of the guard station and pushed the button. I had been told to never push the button unless it was an absolute emergency. I had been in the hell on earth for almost 24 hours and it was an emergency to me to get as far away from this place as possible. "Yeah" was the command that blurted out from the distorted speaker.

In my most intelligent, gracious, humble and meek voice I responded, "This is my first time here and I was told that I would be appearing before the judge today, sir. Can you check on that for me, please?"

The obviously annoyed voice on the other end responded harshly and to the point. "If you are scheduled, then we will call you when it's time."

"And what time is that, kind sir?" I retorted.

The speaker went dead and so did my spirits. I retreated to my cell with my head held high, but my pride hung low like rotting fruit in an orchard. I fell asleep once again, hoping that when I awoke this nightmare would be over. I awoke to hear the guard trying to pronounce names like he never made it past third grade, stumbling and bumbling on the simplest of surnames. He pronounced my name "Priston" but that was fine with me as I scurried to get up, wash my face off, and get the process started of putting this nightmare behind me. One by one we were directed into the sally port, the area between the guard station and the housing unit, as our identification bands were checked and verified. We were instructed to sit on a series of benches that sat up from ground level like a shoe-shiner's chair rising above its patrons at most international airports in America. The trustees rolled up with those same carts that just some nineteen hours ago held bedrolls now were draped with steel as in shackles and handcuffs. This couldn't really be happening, could it?

One each of the apparatus was thrown at the feet of each one of us as it slid into its perfect resting place, like schoolboys pitching pennies against a bathroom wall. As the cold steel came to its resting place, a skilled officer grabbed the medieval-looking jewelry and skillfully clasped the cuffs around my ankles; inserting a key that looked like a tiny screwdriver, he turned it clockwise and waited to hear the click of the locking mechanism before doing the same to each one of my wrists. "Stand up and follow me" was the command that echoed in the cold and empty halls of the prison. Standing to my feet was more easily said than done, but I managed to stand erect and follow my captors. I wanted this over more than any boring movie, standardized test, or long-winded sermon.

Like cattle being led to slaughter, we slowly and methodically made our way to the elevator. We were packed into the landing like sardines and swiftly lowered to the ground level into a large hallway marked with grey stripes and steel doors identifiable in red "For Administration Only." I noticed a clock on the wall and it read 5:30. The hearing was to begin at 9:00 so I was much obliged to see that the judge saw fit to get in early and take care of me, because I deserved better. It seemed like an endless stream of humanity stepping off the elevator. They were from the sixth floor to the second floor, male and female, black and white. Some were in wheelchairs; others had crutches while some were missing arms or legs. Blind men were not excluded from this most sacred fraternity as well as the deaf and mute; this was a subculture lost in obscurity to most but known to the criminal justice system on a first-name basis.

After dividing us according to whether we had committed a felony or a misdemeanor, we were led past yet another control room and put into holding cells the size of a walk in closet and packed in like luggage in the bottom of a Greyhound bus. The door was locked. Some of us stood up while others sat down on the stone-hard and ice-cold benches with their heads hanging low like rotting fruit on a tree. Most remained silent while others talked about their cases. The war stories in that room were no match for ones that I had heard from my dad who was a World War II veteran. The stench of funky men, cold steel, and pee filled the place. The scene was horrible, humiliating, and humbling to put it mildly.

After about three hours of this hell, the door finally opened and we were called out one by one and led into the court-room like cattle to slaughter. As I passed from the steel drab grey walls of concrete to the colorful world of walnut-colored walls and shiny veneer benches, it was surreal. It took several moments for my eyes to adjust to the incandescent light. This was a beautiful world with pictures hanging on the wall, the Stars and Stripes flying next to the state flag of Florida, the smell of coffee emanating from mugs, a clock. I had literally passed from the land of the dead into the land of hope and promise, and my hope was to let justice be served, pay my debt to society (albeit not behind bars), and get on with my life.

There was a throng of people moving about the court-room. The stenographer was setting up what seemed to be her mobile shorthand typewriter, as court clerks organized large manila file folders. They worked in concert like ants building a mound. The young, suave, and debonair state's attorney was handsomely dressed in an Italian wool pinstriped suit that was beautifully matched with a paisley tie, matching handkerchief, and French cuffs. The fair and lovely public defender was a long, slender blonde with flowing locks, ruby-red lipstick and curves more pronounced than a Formula One racetrack. Her black dress gently hugged her curvaceous body, and a string of pearls dangled from her neck. She was prim, proper, pretty, and professional. This stateroom also had its share of police presence, with real cops and real guns loaded into holsters.

At the back of the courtroom, just like on television, the audience filed in one by one. As each inmate caught a glimpse of his or her loved one, an awkward shackled wave of sorts was exchanged between the accused and the free. One of the officers stood, gathered everyone's attention, and quickly gave us all the details on how we should conduct ourselves in the proceedings. He asked if we all understood, because this was our one and only warning--violators would be removed from the forum and escorted back upstairs until the next proceeding. No, please don't throw me in the briar patch. Alas, I saw my dad and brother ease into their seats as I tried my best to wave in my iron bracelets. I was ecstatic to see them but sad that they were seeing me hog-tied like a calf in a rodeo. Feelings of guilt and shame ravaged through my already guilt-ridden mind. I wanted to pray. I didn't pray anymore at night because I thought that no one heard them, so why would this be any different?

After the officer finished his announcements and threats, the sounds of people talking and whispering filled the air once again. All of a sudden the sound of wood slapping against wood silenced everyone with the bailiff bellowing, "All rise." A tall, silver-haired man in a black robe entered from a door behind the vaulted judge's bench and sat down immediately.

We were then asked to raise our right hand, to the best of our ability, and repeat after him.

"Do you promise to tell the whole truth and nothing but the truth so help me God?"

"I do," we all said in unison.

Who says no? I wondered. The judge explained our plea options. We could either confess (guilty) and take our punishment, plead not guilty and be sent back upstairs for a court date that was weeks away, or enter a plea of no contest or nolo contendere. This concedes the charges alleged without disputing or admitting guilt and without offering a defense. Going back upstairs was not an option that I was considering. As the proceedings got underway, I was amazed by the untruths that my counterparts had been spewing for the last 24 hours. For example, one guy who resided only two cells down from me had been staunchly committed to the fact that he was wrongly accused of the crime for which he was arrested, and that crime was driving on a suspended license. However, when his charges were read aloud for the whole world to hear, the truth came to light. Since this was only first appearance court, we were spared the sick and grisly details of the probable cause that kept him detained, but he was ultimately charged with having sex with a minor.

My charges, although criminal, in my mind were less egregious, because I hurt no one, or so I thought. When my name was finally called to approach the bench, the charges were read in full. I was charged with thirteen counts of obtaining property with a worthless check less than $150. My father asked if he could speak and was granted the opportunity to come stand beside his son. He ignored me and we never made eye contact. He had the look of a puzzled man, the look of a man who had put his very soul and spirit into rearing a child and was suddenly let down. I had never felt so much disconnect from him in my life. He had his Kangol hat, which he was known to wear, in one hand as he addressed the judge. I was happy that he hadn't abandoned me, yet sad that it had come to my father being by my side in a Florida state court of law.

He spoke on my behalf and gave the judge his word that this would never happen again and he would make sure that all fines and restitution would be paid back to the state. He never looked my way again. He was ashamed and truly puzzled as to why an able-bodied man who went to work every day and earned a wage that was more than he had ever earned while delivering mail for thirty-seven years, and had six fewer kids than he, could stoop so low, essentially stealing from others with no regard for their feelings or the consequences that came along with committing such a callous act. The judge asked me how I wanted to plead to my crimes.

This was going faster than I had expected so I paused, looked around the courtroom and without reservation said, "Your honor, I plead the way that will get me home faster."

The room erupted in laughter. The public defender came to my rescue and whispered in my ear explaining my options. "I would like to enter a plea of guilty your honor." With that, he sentenced me to one year of probation and a promise to pay restitution to my victims. He also mentioned paying fines, court costs, and fees associated with the bad instruments that I had passed at the said retailers. At this point I would have agreed to going ten rounds with Muhammad Ali blindfolded.

He banged his gavel and called out the next name. I was whisked into an adjoining room only to be fingerprinted again and registered for probation, which included the stipulations most of which I knew that I could not adhere to. No drinking, no drugs, no visitation to establishments that offer the two, reporting to the probation office once a month, and paying $40 just for the privilege to be a free man-- and paying back all those fines, which totaled in the thousands of dollars. I gave affirmative responses to all the demands of my captors--please just remove these shackles, return my civilian clothes, and let me breathe some fresh air. After signing all of the necessary documents I raised my arm so these menacing manacles could be removed, only to be laughed at and then led out the door and back into the direction from whence I had come some hours ago. This was not like an episode of Perry Mason where once the case has been resolved, the families embrace, shed a tear or two, then convene at the closest steakhouse.

I walked down that same lonely, cold hallway to that same guy at the control booth, got on that same elevator only to be catapulted up to that same unit to that same cell to that same foolishness. Hey man, what happened? Are you going home today? Can I have your lunch? Give me this. Give me that. I was informed by the guards that if I was indeed freed that it would take a minimum of fourteen hours just to process me out, and that by law they could keep me up until 11:59 p.m. And what did they mean, "if"? This was a mind game that Dr. Frankenstein could have only concocted in black-and-white science fiction movies. The mental torture of not knowing was unbearable. The mind game of the unknown was barbaric. I climbed into my rack and tried to sleep my time away, but each sound roused me from my slight slumber. I was a broken man, but a man who was now longing for a cold beer and a celebratory joint. The covenant that I had proposed to God was slipping away word by word as each minute to freedom ticked away. The names were called over the loudspeaker: "Jones, Culpepper, Wisnoski, Aspinwall, pack it up." Those were the three words that I needed to hear. Finally, around 5 p.m., right before feeding time, the name Preston was called in a nearly inaudible, faint whisper. I would have missed it but they also called my cell number.

I sprang to my feet like a gymnast going for gold in the Olympics. The big blue door slid back at a snail's pace as the inmates bum's-rushed me to ask for what was left of my personal effects, including my used toothbrush and comb. The officer on duty checked my armband and although my smile was as wide as the Okeefeenoke swamp he looked unaffected by my joy. I made my way out the same way I came in, going through a series of checkpoints as I was directed by officers strategically placed about the facility. I finally made it to Utopia, releasing read the sign on the wall. A long line of fellow inmates waited along the wall as I took my place on the track. It was the same boundary that I had followed into this armpit of hell, and it marked the spot to begin my release. Some of the faces were familiar ones that I had seen being booked the day before and some agonized with me in the cramped holding cell before court began more than twenty-four hours ago. We were instructed to be on our best behavior and that talking was forbidden.

As each inmate was called to the releasing window, they

were given a brown paper bag and personal items that had been inventoried on the other side of the jail were now being given back to the owner of the property. In a morbid and sick way, it was like a processing plant, but instead of raw product entering into one end of the plant and the finished product exiting the facility, they did it with humans and the biggest difference was the finished product. Was I now refined? Was I better than when I entered? Did the process make me better?

My name was finally called and after observing the procedure for more than two hours, I knew the drill. Step to the line, toss linen and blanket into cart, come back to window, read wristband, sign off for personal effects, go to bathroom and change into civilian clothes, don't steal their socks, line up on the opposite side of the hallway and wait some more. Tom Petty's hit "The Waiting Is the Hardest Part" played over and over in my head as I vowed never to return to this horrible place. My clothes, after being balled up in a grocery sack were more wrinkled than a 100-year-old man and were as stale as week-old bread, but they felt like a hand-sewn Italian suit to me at the moment. There around the last corner where I thought my previous incarcerates had left to enjoy their freedom stood yet another holding cell with familiar faces waiting with bated breath to leave lockup. If not for my juxtaposition, a man who is not supposed to cry, and a man in jail who better not cry, I would have shed enough tears to fill a water well. This was the cell where all the "when I get out of here" stories were being told. Some had wild dreams of having sex, eating a steak, or "hitting a lick" (when translated for the hip impaired simply means to "do dirt" or engage in more criminal activity, or simplified to its simplest terms, they were making reservations for future stays at the less-than-one-star hotel).

I just wanted not to be at the mercy of another man. Period. I said prayers in my mind and thanked God for letting me live through this. Another hour and my name was called; once again I had figured out the procedure by watching and longing for it to be me. "What is your date of birth? What is your father's name? What is your current address?" asked the officer through a window that surprisingly had no bars or glass. They could have asked me the square root of 5698 and I was prepared to answer correctly.

One last check of the armband--and with a snip of the scissors it dropped into her hand like shackles falling from a slave. She pointed eastward and informed me that she would buzz me out. We were out of synchronization on the first try as my adrenaline was flowing like the mighty Mississippi River at flood levels. We tried it again, I could hear the buzz and the click of the lock making beautiful music like Simon and Garfunkel, Sonny and Cher, or Bach and Beethoven. I pulled on that door with all my might and made my way from the dark to the light with my teeth shimmering in the sunlight. I had made a promise to God that if He would get me out of this situation, I would get my life in order, stop drinking and getting high, and be a better human being, but I never promised to give myself to God and in not doing so, I would make this return trip over twenty-seven times in the next fifteen years.

CHAPTER 6
Intent to Deceive

If hyperbole is exaggeration with no intention to deceive, co-caine is just the opposite. Its sole intent is to do just that, and that was its allure to me. It had become my first, my last, my everything. When I was doing it my only thought was how to get more and never run out, and when I wasn't doing it my only thought was to do it. The desire to partake in this com-pulsion lived inside me as a quasi-entity or subpersonality, an energy field that took me over completely. It was even taking over my mind, the voice in my head, which was the voice of addiction, saying, "You've had a rough day. You deserve a treat. Why deny yourself the only pleasure that is left in your life?" Sure, my life was falling apart like a house made of straw, but it was my house, and that was all that mattered to me. I became a house husband, although I wasn't married, as Courtney's mother assumed the arduous task of caring for two babies, one of them in his late twenties.

Temporary agencies were in their infancy, so I decided to give them a try. I met with one of their recruiters and she eventually decided on assignment that was in need of a guy such as myself with a science and mathematics background. The company was an aerospace company that manufactured ignition systems for aircraft engines. When I entered their complex, which was located a few blocks from the insurance company, I was in awe of the sheer enormity of the company. There was a series of tan brick buildings nestled between 100-year-old trees that had beards of Spanish moss hanging from them, like soldiers in the Civil War. As I parked, off in the distance were huge tanks that looked like the solid rocket boosters that flank on either side of the space shuttle during take-off, marked "Danger: Liquid Nitrogen." I parked away from the human resources building so I could get a glimpse of everything that was in view. Some of the structures were higher than others; they were connected by cylindrical-shaped tunnels that reminded me of the tanks of sea life at an aquarium. I noticed that everyone who entered did so by using a magnetic card reader, sliding it from left to right in the scanner and waiting for the small illuminated light to change from red to green to signal entry. This was state-of-the-art technology in the early '90s—no, this was beyond that; it was James Bond come to life technology.

I was thrilled at the opportunity afforded before me and I made up in my disturbed mind that I was going to get my foot in the door and then just like James brown says, "just open the door, I'll get it myself." I made my way through the throng of workers; some had on light-blue smocks with the name of the company stenciled above the upper left pen pocket, and some had on shirt and tie with their identification badge and their picture with a 6-digit employee number tucked neatly in their shirt pocket. I surmised that the folks not in a shirt and tie did more of a manual labor type of job, so I reasoned, in my diseased brain, that I would be wearing a tie and not a smock. I was met with a smile by the HR representative even though I was just a temporary. I surveyed the situation as I waited for my supervisor to come and escort me to the department that I was selected to help out. This was going much better than I had anticipated, but in the back of my mind I kept feeling that my dream job dream would be interrupted by someone from the janitorial services waltzing through that door with a bio-hazard suit and gas mask and asking me, "Are you allergic to plutonium?" Although I had never in my life been a pessi-mist, it was a time in my life that I had every right to question myself. Hell, I was losing jobs faster than a toddler loses his toys, my drinking level was higher than the Hillary step, and I was smoking the most addictive substance known to man. But other than that, I was okay.

I met my supervisor for the first time as he came to take me to my work area. He was a thin man with wire-rimmed glasses, he spoke with an upstate New York accent, and he was very animated. In fact, he was so animated that he re-minded me of a cartoon character, but I noticed that he had a short-sleeved dress shirt and a tie on for his work uniform. He also had a pocket protector with many pens and other ap-paratus in his left pocket and contrary to popular belief, deep down I was a nerd at heart. A black Bill Nye the Science Guy. I was overflowing with emotion, anxiety, and joy but I kept them in check just in case he was just there to escort me to the Custodial Technicians Department.

As we left the administrative offices in the huge building,

things got even more interesting. Our small journey would take us by a myriad of different departments that made this industrial giant tick. First we passed the machine shop, where I could see a dozen or so ladies and gentlemen boring, lathing, drilling reaming and milling on state-of-the-art equipment that was every bit sophisticated as it was rugged. A few paces from this noisy and exposed area we found the likes of the Metrology Lab. Metrology is defined by the International Bureau of Weights and Measurements (BIPM) as "the science of measurement, embracing both experimental and theoretical determinations at any level of uncertainty in any field of science of technology." Vernier calipers, microscopes, and micrometers were the pens and pencils used in this modern marvel. We visited the quality department next, which was a smaller extension of the metrology lab or "First Article," as it was called by my boss. If you had ever wondered why you had to take the physical sciences in school, then this place would quickly answer that question only leaving you wondering, "Did I take enough?"

We walked down cavernous hallways and at each turn there was someone assembling something. Huge cables comprised of dozens of smaller wires laid on pre-diagrammed boards like giant anacondas in a controlled rainforest. There were warning signs of every shape, color, and size to keep workers from disaster. The noises that permeated throughout the plant resembled the jungle as well, as timers buzzed like a team of insects in a swamp, and fans roared like small mammals. The smell of smelted metals wafted through the air like a burnt meal on Thanksgiving. We stopped by the cafeteria to pick up a couple of cold drinks as we continued on our fascinating trek.

Next stop was the coil-winding area were workers, most of them women, took magnetic coils and used a state-of-the-art machine to wind loops of wire through the center the loop where an electric current was passed through the wire to generate a magnetic field. Don't wake me, I must be dreaming. As we passed through the production area of the building, he explained to me that they were assembling exciters. Ignition exciters are available for virtually any main propulsion or auxiliary power units. He went on to say that they, exciters, were like the solid state ignition system in an automobile; they played an integral part in starting the engine of airplanes. This was getting better by the minute. Once we made it to the engineering department, I was introduced to several engineers, CAD designers, technicians, and quality- control managers. We made our way through one of the many doors and finally came to a rest at a place called Experimental. I would soon learn that before any one of their many products went to full-blown production, sample units were first built in small numbers and rigorously tested to Federal Aviation Administrators standards.

So where would I come into play? I asked myself over and over again in my mind. He explained to me, to the best of his ability, that I would be an expediter. This person would be in charge of procuring parts, FAA inspections, obtaining process engineering flow charts, and updating the drawings for each part used to make the final product as well as the final product itself. I was awestruck, dumbfounded, and ecstatic all at the same time. In my mind I knew I was more than capable of doing an exemplary job, but in my heart--usually where it counts most of all--I was unsure of myself. I was actively participating in a reckless and dangerous lifestyle... I had no clue to where it was going to lead me, I seemed to have no control over it, and it was out to kill me.

I took to this job like a duck to water. I was always on time and excited about the new and refreshing challenges that each day held. My sole intent was to show my worth to the company and that I should be hired on permanently. I was starting to develop business as well as personal relationships with some of the most influential people in the company. It was not uncommon to see me at happy hour with the vice president of the engineering department or throwing down beers with the lead engineers of some of the biggest projects in the company. I had also drawn near to my two assemblers for the experimental department, Gary and Pam. Gary was a cool, stylishly dressed black man about ten years my senior. He had served in the Navy and was originally from Steubenville, Ohio. He was quiet, methodical, and highly regarded in the engineering department. Pam was just the opposite: she was a brash, fun-loving woman with a southern charm. She loved to joke around and have fun. She was divorced with a teenaged daughter. She was full of life, full of spirit and full of—well, fill in the blank. We both were Jacksonville natives and shared many stories and experiences.

Gary, Pam, and I formed the perfect team. Both of them knew that I longed for the position and I must say they, along with my supervisor, became my biggest advocates. I was a team player, a positive attitude fueled me, and I went the extra mile. Being a temporary employee, I would be excluded from the much-celebrated windfall but it was just one more jaw- dropping benefit offered by this would-be dream job.

My supervisor, in sworn secrecy, confided that he had been in contact with the vice president of human relations and that at the beginning of the year, a temporary to full-time position was imminent. I was elated--this was not only my dream job but it was a dream job at which I had worked diligently, professionally, and dutifully to even be considered a viable candidate. All I would have to do is fill out the new hire paperwork, benefits package...and oh, did I mention a drug test? I had approximately three weeks to clean out a system that had more toxins in it than Three Mile Island. I was a cesspool of cocaine, crack and marijuana residue but I had three weeks to change twenty years of self- induced trauma. I was approaching thirty and had been an alcoholic since age six, a chronic dug user since adolescence--no problem!

Over the holidays I tried to scale back my drug usage. I would not be tested for alcohol, so I drank more. It would be foolhardy of me to say that I traded one for the other because that would imply that I gave one up. This may sound crazy, and it is--I smoked more crack and snorted more cocaine than marijuana because coke doesn't stay in the system as long as THC and I would have a better chance of "beating" the test, not passing it. When we returned from the break, I knew in my heart that I would test positive for something but there was bad/good news. My manager informed me that there was a delay in plans and that the hiring was pushed back a few weeks. In my sick mind I rejoiced over the delay and once again rationalized that it would give me even more time to get it together. Do I need to give you the definition of insanity, or are you already there?

It was business as usual for me. My insatiable need to get

high and drunk was overshadowing everything in my life. My values were dwindling like sand in an hourglass, my convictions were as shaky as a two-legged stool, and my morals were as stinky as seafood left in a parked car for eight hours in July. It was January 31st, and almost four weeks had elapsed since returning from the Christmas break, when I was summoned into his office. Gary, Pam, and a bevy of engineers that I had befriended over my "internship" were there to revel in unison at what was supposed to be my crowning achievement. I was about to be one of them not just in spirit but now as a true brother. The adoption would now be finalized, the unbiblical cord cut, and the guy with all the ambition, talent, and charisma would flourish and rise to the top. I was happy but not overjoyed because I knew that the night before had been a humdinger. And for the sake of keeping it real, the past month had been a humdinger. I had probably smoked more and snorted more substances in that small period of time than in the previous year combined. After the cake was eaten, the congratulations extended, and balloons popped, I asked my soon-to-be overseer, "When do I take my physical?" This was just another example of my mastery of manipulation, because I knew that physical really meant drug screening.

Margaret was the secretary for the vice president of human resources, and he had made an appointment for me to see her tomorrow. The department invited everyone out to happy hour to celebrate my invitation to join the elite. Although I had every intention of going home and beginning my mass internal cleaning, I had the bright idea to ask each person in the crowd for a small loan until I got my first real paycheck, and they responded like champs. I probably walked out of that bar with a net take of over two hundred dollars. Drunk, I drove as fast as I could to the "spot" and added more fuel to the forest fire called Richard. After finally coming home broke, drunk, and high, I exclaimed to my family that all of our worries would soon be over because I had just struck it big and would soon be bringing home a paycheck that would essentially double my salary and eventually double my pain.

I arrived at Margaret's office a quarter to seven--I prided myself on being on time. She had all the usual paperwork for a new hire to fill out: a W-4, an I-9, and benefits packages to choose from. She offered me a cup of coffee, which I graciously accepted to mask the smell of the beer that I drank on the drive down Interstate 95. She took my picture for my much-coveted employee badge with the company's logo and my very own ID number on it. This process was picking up steam like a train ready to leave the station. I signed what she said would be my last form and then the dreaded words that I knew were coming but I didn't want to hear--"This is your drug testing kit." I heard those six words and nothing more. An emptiness that was hidden by the smile on my face lay at the bottom of my stomach. I asked my God, whom I had not been particularly familiar with as of late, to help me. Because even in my altered state of mind, I knew that he was really the only one who could.

Then suddenly as I was leaving after my half-hearted prayer, she said, "Just report to the specified lab within 72 hours."

My prayer was answered. I now had 72 hours to undo, fix, change--or whatever you want to call it--72 months of fierce partying. I drank water like a man who had been stranded on the Gobi Desert and I invested in goldenseal, a part of American folklore associated with chemical testing. It aids in digestion and hence it is widely believed that it speeds up metabolism, getting chemicals out of the body sooner and masking the byproducts. I doubled up on the seals and doubled down on the dope. I tried to not do any drugs at all, but they seemed to find me. Friends, neighbors and even strangers were reaching out to me with free hits. The rationalization in my head to even pick up a drug was overwhelming. For every negative on getting high, my brain would supply five positives on why it was okay to indulge. When I arrived at the laboratory for one of the most important tests of my life, I was nervous but confident. Somehow I managed not to smoke or ingest any type of illegal narcotic into my body the night before. I had thought of cheating on the test by using some of my daughter's or her mother's urine--but that would be cheating, and believe it or not I still considered myself to have high moral standards. Go figure.

The next day after submitting to the urinalysis, I reported to work beaming with confidence. I had my game face on and felt good about myself. I went over the benefits package with Gary and Pam and discussed the 401k options in an effort not only to ease my mind, but to somehow breathe confidence and positivity into the aura surrounding the situation. In other words, I was scared to death about the entire situation. I knew deep down in my inner craw that if I passed that screening, it was all a sham anyway. The next few days at work were going so well that I sort of forgot about my impending results. I was working on the Pratt and Whitney 500 program, a series of medium-thrust turbofan engines designed specifically for business jet applications. I was putting in hours of overtime to make sure that the product would be delivered to the customer on time. We, the engineering team, finished the product on schedule and delivered a superior product that earned all of us a well-deserved round of applause from the owner, Rick Sontag, himself. We went out to happy hour to celebrate the victory and as usual I had my fill and somebody else's fill too.

The next day I was nursing a hangover when I heard my name called over the public address system, which typically was not unusual, but it was not from coil winding, or production, or Gary inviting me to lunch...it was from the human resources secretary, Margaret. My heart dropped into my stomach. I might be a drug addict, but I was no fool... well, I was, but you get the point. Although the HR department was only minutes from the engineering department, it was one of the longest and loneliest walks that I had ever taken. Margaret met me at the door. She was a tall, slender, middle-aged blonde who certainly could have been a model in her younger years. She wore a snug form-fitted skirt that accentuated her long legs. She moved with grace and elegance and usually had a matching sweater, to accompany her outfit, tied loosely around her neck. She was smiling as usual and motioned for me to go into the office of the vice president of human resources, Mr. Nielsen. I took a deep breath and tried everything in my power to calm my nerves, all the time rehearsing my "I lost another job speech" to tell to Courtney and her mother.

I slowly turned the knob and pulled on the door when all that was required was a push. The first face that I encountered was Rick Landers, the director of engineering. He was a short fellow with rosy cheeks, who already seemed to be speculative about me anyway; he was known not only for engineering prowess, but for his vast array of short-sleeved dress shirts that matched his collection of clip on ties perfectly. Seated next to him was my boss and seated behind a vintage, mid-century antique desk was Mr. Nielsen himself. He shook my hand with a firmness I would expect from an executive and motioned for me to have a seat in the vacant seat next to his desk. I could barely look my manager in the face because he was the man responsible for my being here in the first place. He was the lone soul that believed in me since day one; he was the guy who put his reputation on the line to back me for this important position--he was the teacher and I was the pupil, he was my master and I was his grasshopper.

Mr. Nielsen wasted no time. He began by saying exactly why I was there. "Richard, you have failed to live up to your minimum obligations set forth by our company. Your drug screen has detected trace amounts of THC and cannabis." I chuckled inside because I knew they were just being diplomatic by using the term "trace."

I also wondered in my mind why we were at such a formal forum to announce to a temporary employee that he screwed up one of his biggest opportunities to date. My eyes were fixated on the huge Unison logo on the wall as he started to recognize some of my accomplishments since coming to the company in a temporary capacity. He went on to say how I was well respected and my potential for success was huge. The accolades began to rain down like an afternoon thundershower in July. This was turning out to be the most cordial and sophisticated firing to date. As he continued, my mind drifted to my list of failures. They were starting to pile up like dirty dishes in the sink of a bachelor's pad. I reeled myself in from this impromptu daydream and began listening attentively again to his narrative, which was turning out to be very different than my last FUBARs, and then as smoothly as a Cadillac shifting gears, Mr. Nielsen said, "Now if this was cocaine that we are talking about, we would be not having this discussion."

What discussion? I looked at my boss and he smiled at me and nodded in the direction of what I thought was my executioner as if to say, "Wait, there's more." Mr. Nielsen tugged at the shiny gold cuff links that protruded from the sleeve of his French cuffed dress shirt, adjusted his reading glasses to the bridge of his nose, looked me squarely in both eyes and said, "Although I would, of course, not be here today discussing this matter, but it is in my judgement based upon your work results, interviews with some of your fellow co-workers, personal results ,and this man's rave review of you, we are going to offer you the position of materials coordinator in our engineering department."

There was silence in the room. You could hear a fly urinating on cotton. He went on to say that there would be a few stipulations that would carry grave consequences if breached. First, I would be drug tested, randomly, for the next year at least once a month. Secondly, if I were to be suspected of being impaired on the job, I would be immediately terminated without question. And thirdly, which I believe was of most concern to the company, I was to tell absolutely no one of the events that just transpired in this office. Numbers two and three would be a cinch, because who would I tell--and really, who would believe such a story in today's liability-law-suit-driven climate? Being suspected of being impaired was a joke because at the time that they made that ultimatum, I was impaired.

At this moment, I remember saying, "Thank God," but it was just callously used because, after all, isn't that what I was supposed to say? I would later learn different.

The job was going well and as my tenure and performance increased, so did my salary and my usage. My daughter's mother eventually kicked me to the curb after several incidences of unexplained absences from home, and paydays where every cent of my money was unaccounted-for. I was now smoking a mixture of crack and weed on a daily basis. Crack had become a cheap, street corner drug sold in the heart of the inner city, eating away at the most vulnerable people in the center of the most socioeconomically deprived areas of cities in the United States. It was highly profitable, easy to make, and for some of its dealers, it was a way to get rich at your neighbor's expense. It was a modern-day genocide driven by money, money and more money. Crack was known to be mixed with battery acid, drain cleaner, lye, and pot ash, but it was so addictive none of its users ever bothered to read the Surgeon General's warning on the label. Babies were being born addicted in the womb, as their mother was unable to kick the habit during pregnancy. These babies were termed "crack babies" and they began life lacking in cognitive skills, brain development, and physical ability. Many had to endure long hospital stays and had to be weaned off narcotics before they would ever see the light of day. Young black males and females were being killed in record numbers as turf wars, shady deals, and robberies transformed the black community into literal war zones. New words and terms came about as a result of the drug. Carjacking and home invasions, and drive-bys are just some of the terms derived as a direct byproduct of the drug's popularity and propensity for crime.

If I were to describe the switch, jump, progression or graduation to this insanity, let's just say it would be like going from the fire to nuclear fission. If you are not aware of the power of this man-made phenomenon, let me try to enlighten you a bit. The amount of free energy contained in nuclear fuel is millions of times the amount of free energy contained in a similar mass of chemical fuel such as gasoline, making it a very dense source of energy, and you can say the same about cocaine versus crack. I was now dealing with a very dense, dark, destructive substance. Ironically, the switch happened one day when I was not able to score some weed. I was doing, well I thought I was doing quite well when I was just "juicing" joints. Anyway, on a typical day after work, I went to procure the two ingredients for my after-work cocktail, weed and crack. I say them in that order because that is usually the sequence in which I bought them, but on this day I ran into the Crackman first and he offered me a "blessing" as they would say. I proceeded to get the weed, but the "trap" was getting raided.

Now if one is not familiar with the comings and goings of the "hood," allow me to elucidate. When one dope house is raided, word spreads like Peter Pan on Merita bread, and operations are shut down until "nine," the police, has wrapped up their investigation and moved on. The community is now considered "hot" and all the dealers are paranoid. So here I was in my dope quandary; my mind was saying, "Just save the stuff until tomorrow, it will be okay," but my body was saying, "Are you kidding me? You worked hard for that dope--why put off until tomorrow what you can do today?" In Sigmund Freud's structural model of the psyche where the ego is the organized, realistic part that mediates between the desires of the id and the superego, the id is the set of uncoordinated instinctual trends; the superego plays the critical and moralizing role; and the ego is the organized, realistic part that mediates between the desires of the id and the superego. The superego can stop one from doing certain things that one's id may want to do. At this stage of my addiction, that had crept up on me like a child playing peek -a- boo, the id was winning the debate in most every case lately.

I had witnessed some of the "crack girls" doing their thing in times of other indiscretions in my life. I recalled how they, the prostitutes, smoked the stuff on top of a beer can, but I couldn't remember how they fastened the apparatus to be user-friendly. I dug deep into my mind and began to reenact the scene. First, I needed a twelve-ounce beer can, so I quickly went to the fridge and drank the contents as I pondered my next move. I knew I needed some sort of ventilation so that the smoke could be drawn into my mouth. Aha--the girls always had safety pins at their disposal. I ran upstairs and scrounged through my dresser and found a needle from a sewing kit; this was going to have to do. I poked several holes in the top of the can and crushed the can together like an aluminum accordion. I placed the crack on top of the can, and not wanting to waste my prized piece, I surveyed the situation and surmised that something was missing. It needed something to help burn it, and I suddenly remembered how all those chicks smoked cigarettes and would place ashes over the holes as an incendiary source. I had no smokes. As crazy as this may sound, I despised the smoking of tobacco. It had no "get high" value to me, they were expensive, a waste of time and energy and get this, harmful to your health.

I walked up to Happy Jacks Groceries, which was located at the corner of Grothe and Myrtle. This corner was a veritable outside market for the sale and procurement of illicit and illegal drugs. I walked the gauntlet of young, "grilled-up," gold-chain-wearing, pants sagging, disrespectful, money rolled up in their fist, no-shoestring-wearing, wife beater-playing, gun-toting, bicycle-riding, speech-slurring dudes, all of whom asked me consecutively, "Are you straight?" I politely declined each invitation and made my way up to the counter and asked for a "loose cigarette." These are single smokes sold, imagine this, illegally in most of America's challenged neighborhoods. I bought a dollar's worth and prepared myself to go through the same combat zone from which I had come. Back at home, the can was sitting on the table and the hole from which the liquids are designed to pour was facing me, and positioned in a way as if to say, "wait'll you get a load of me."

I made my ashes and gently scooped them out of the ashtray with a folded matchbook cover. The process made me feel like I was back in Mr. Saffer's physics class at Sandalwood. I spread them carefully over the holes like I was spreading a loved one's remains over a sacred area. I placed a small sample piece on the crest of the ashes. I "flicked my Bic" and rotated the lighter about 55 degrees to obtain the perfect fire to dope ratio. The poison began to sizzle, like French fries being added to hot grease, but on a smaller scale. I put my mouth over the hole in the can, inhaled and awaited my fate. Although I had never smoked "straight" crack before, I knew the danger as evidenced by the gauntlet that I had just walked, as evidenced by women riding around the neighborhood at 3:00 am soliciting their drawn up and stinky bodies for $10, as evidenced by a crime rate that doubled since the "dawn of crack," as evidenced by babies being born underdeveloped and addicted, as evidenced by fallen comrades who had succumbed to the drug's powerful stronghold, but I chose to challenge its toughness because I was the mighty Richard Preston and I was invincible.

The smoke hit my lungs like a boxer hitting the big bag. I froze in an instant and gazed around the room in wonderment. The earth seemed to stand still and the silence of the moment was uncanny. I wasn't sure of what I was feeling, but there was one thing that I was sure of at that moment and it was that I had been wasting my money on weed. I could hear, at first, bells ringing silently in my ears and then that faded to a faint, hollow emptiness as if I were in a vacuum. Then my hearing achieved a super sensitivity, and it seemed as if I could hear things from miles away. I could sense someone's presence, but I knew that I was the only one in the room. I gently put the can down like a jeweler handling fine diamonds and went to the front door and looked out--no one. I then went to the back door and did the same...no one, I went upstairs, no one, peeked out the blinds, still nobody. I went back to the "office" and partook in another blast of my newfound love. Not unlike the people who had claimed to have out-of-body experiences, I felt like I was suspended somewhere between earth and heaven not realizing that my hell on earth had just begun.

I was "faking the funk" pretty well at work, as I was living a double life. I was a full- blown "baser" at night and a materials coordinator for the largest manufacturer of aircraft engine ignition systems in the world by day, and my job was an important one. Before any parts were put into production, they were built in my experimental department and it was my job to follow its build from idea to blueprints, to procurement, to process, to assembly, to FAA inspection. Approximately 90 percent of my projects found their way to some of the most advanced engines in the aviation field and I did an exemplary job with dope flowing through my bloodstream like hemoglobin. I could speak to anyone in the plant from the owner to the shipping personnel and engage in a conversation that was on their level. I also kept in the back of my mind that at any time I could be drug tested and that would be the end of this cool 50k a year job.

I maintained a positive image for years cloaked under a dark cloud of chaos. My car was in need of maintenance, my refrigerator was bare, and like Stevie Wonder sings in his song "Living for the City," "my clothes were old but never were they dirty." I was bumming money from the more than forty engineers and technicians that needed my services to get projects started, approved and completed on time. As I look back, I was running a sort of project- completion scam, for lack of a better term. Because the closer that particular person's due date neared, I found it easier to hit him or her up for "lunch or gas money." I was also able to talk my way into getting credit from the dope boys because they saw me go to work each morning and they had brains enough to know when I got paid, they in turn got paid.

There were times when I literally owed them my entire check because the prime lending rate on the street is 100 percent. They would give you $100 dollars' worth of dope and instantly you owed $200; they capitalized on addiction better than any lending institution in America governed by the FDIC. I began over drawing my checking account, writing more bad checks, and I discovered a way to channel funds from my 401k. I convinced Kelly, who was our benefits specialist, that I was constantly about to be evicted and I would draft false letters and sign my brother's name to the document in question. Kelly was a slender, caring lady who always wore a tan sweater and smoked probably more than she should have. I don't know if she believed each storyline that I came up with as each one got more dramatic than the previous one, but she always came through as I quickly used up what was available to me. My life was now a massive game of robbing Peter to pay Paul, with life-altering consequences if the game was not played correctly.

To give you an example, I remember the first time that I knew I had overextended myself and I was not going to make enough to pay back all of the debts, so I got on the offensive and went to one of the guys to buy more time. He was leaning against a payphone between the corner of Grothe and 5th Street on the east side of Myrtle Avenue, smoking a blunt. I told him my circumstance and hoped that he would be the understanding chap that most people would be after hearing the riveting lie that I had just put down on him instead he had a stoic, unemotional look on his face as if to say, "Are you done?"

He never uttered word but instead pulled his shirt up to unveil a huge shiny pistol with a pearl handle and engravings on the side that were too small for me to read, but one thing that I could read was his eyes, and they said it all. I conveniently "moved" some funds around to make sure my date with destiny was not fulfilled at that time. I continued to play Russian Roulette with my life as my addiction took me to lows I never thought imaginable.

I had worked my way up to having an assistant, an answering machine, and the largest office in the process engineering building. It was a prestigious office and I was proud of it as evidenced by my pictures of Courtney, and my football banners from my two favorite football teams, the Washington Redskins and the Miami Hurricanes. We had so much work that my pay grade was changed from salary to salary with overtime--and boy, did I take advantage of this perk. I would work long past my scheduled hours to make more money, buy more drugs, and buy more time from the debt collectors, both legal and illegal. I would sometimes be in the office when the cleaning lady came around to perform her tasks and often talked about one another's children, hobbies, vacations, dreams and aspirations. Little did she know that my dreams were unraveling at the seams like a cheap suit. I even borrowed money from her from time to time even though I knew that she was working two jobs to make a better life for her kids. There was no shame in my game.

I began coming to the job after hours just to be able to eat. I had worked my way up to having the highest security clearance available, which was 24-hour access to the massive buildings. It was then that I started entering after hours and rummaging through the refrigerators in different departments and helping myself to other people's food. I was dining on unfinished Chinese take-out, obscure microwavable dinners, homemade Hungarian goulash, whatever I could find because now food had become a secondary item. I would often go to my mom's house before work and have her make me a plate of whatever was left over from last night's dinner. My colleagues would arrive to work only to find me chowing down on neckbones and lima beans, corned beef and cabbage, or fried chicken and collard greens. I would wash that down with pie, cake, and an ice-cold calorie-laden soft drink.

I recall one morning, Brenda, a materials planner, whose office was just around the corner from me, remarked, "How do you eat all that stuff in the morning and never gain a pound?"

I replied, "Metabolism."

The fact of the matter was; these were the only meals that I was consuming in a 24-hour day. In those days the people were seeing great results with the Slim Fast diet, a shake in a can designed to help the loser shed those ugly unwanted pounds. I was on what was known as the "Stem Fast Diet." A stem is a term used for a pipe used to smoke crack cocaine. This freight train was heading downhill, full speed, with no brakes, knowing certainly that it was eventually going to crash...the only question was when and how bad, and was the crash going to be a fatality. I kept waiting for those random drug tests to start and then I could get some forced help through the Employee Assistance Program and save myself the embarrassment of asking for it, which by the way, would have had the same probability of asking me to voluntarily turn myself into jail. It wasn't going to happen.

So here I was living a double life, a crackhead by night, well-respected employee by day. I was performing at a high clip, achieving the maximum raise each year, but my net worth was zero. I was beginning to get in deep with the dope boys and owing debts that I could not pay. I hid in my house; on some occasions, I had to go hide out at my mother's house. There were times when it would take me hours to smoke a piece of rock that was the size of a #2 pencil eraser because of the time it took me to check each bedroom and look under each bed over and over and over again for fear that someone was in the house with me. Every white car that passed the house took on the image of a police car; every white speck of any material was a piece of crack that I had somehow misplaced or dropped. I would spend countless hours tasting those remnants to see if indeed they were my prized piece of pandemonium. I heard voices coming from inside closets, out in the yard and even in the oven. I saw eyes peeking back at me as I looked tirelessly out of every window in that old house. I was spooked by anything and everything that moved. Guests and visitors were now a thing of the past. I can vividly remember going so far as to lie on the floor and hold my breath in a distorted effort to be stealthy as friends, neighbors, creditors, and even my mother knocked tirelessly at my door.

It was a cool, crisp day in February--the day started like any other, I came in early to eat somebody else's leftovers and to make sure I left home before the sun and people I owed arose. I drank a beer on the way to work and coasted into work on fumes, all the time knowing that I would borrow some money from one of the engineers. It was a Friday and everyone was making plans for the weekend. As I read the newspaper at my desk one of the process engineers, Tony, stopped and shared some bad news. The child of an employee had died suddenly and unexpectedly and he was collecting funds to help the family. I pulled out a crumpled dollar bill that I had used just hours ago to store my stash and handed it over to him and promised that I would find him later to donate more. After finding my pigeon to front me forty dollars for the weekend, I made change and made my way over to see Tony. When I arrived, the well-dressed Filipino man was wearing his signature blue smock over his finely tailored suit. He directed me over to see Marcia, the administrative assistant for the engineers. Marcia was soft-spoken, well- bred, and had a dry sense of humor. She was no-nonsense and was not on my list of people to ask for money. As a matter of fact, it seemed to me that she was always suspicious and leery of me, which if true, made her the smartest of the bunch. I extended one of my borrowed "dubs," the street name for a twenty-dollar bill or a $20 piece of rock, and told her that I would like to contribute to the cause.

She looked at me with a genuine smile and asked, "How much?"

I proudly said, "Five dollars," with the pride of a peacock strutting his feathers, because for me to give over 10 percent of my net worth to any cause was to be applauded. She reached into her desk and pulled out one of those inter office envelopes, the kind that has the six holes for visible confirmation of any contents, string closures, and lines on each side depicting the person(s) and department that the envelope is to be delivered to. She made change and I made note of how much money was packed into the casing. Later that day, I lost the key to my desk and when I called on the maintenance supervisor for entry, he took me to his office and opened a box that was the size of a standard circuit breaker box. He pulled up the number to my lock that coincided with my desk, opened the door to the box and behold, there hung duplicates to every lock on every desk in the building.

Before I continue, I must inform my readers, if you didn't already know, that partaking in the most evil, cunning, sinister, menacing, ominous, baleful, frightening, vile, malevolent, villainous, nefarious, dark substance known to man also comes with the law of unintended circumstances. My addiction had grown to be a gorilla on my back. This weekend was proving to be most difficult, and I was smoking like a broke stove. I did not have food to eat, so I used my security clearance card to enter Unison. I raided the refrigerators from the engineering department to quality control. I found varieties of tasty morsels throughout the building as I rambled through the offices like a raccoon through garbage cans. I found foods of all types, different ethnicities, different tastes, and different levels of expiration. I had come to make this a morbid game of survival as I traversed the expansive building.

As my run of conniving and lying was nearing its end, this old brain that I was convinced was trying to kill me had another revelation. The money that Marcia collected for that grieving family might still be in her desk. I had no intention of stealing it, just using it to get high, and I would replace it before anybody knew the difference. The key box that Paul had inadvertently showed me would be my, pardon the pun, key to entry. I returned to the office, made my way to the box and executed a master plan of debauchery, treachery, deceit--and as my mom would say, just plain old low-down dirty dealing. I never once thought of the magnitude and scope of my actions. I, like most crackheads, thought only of myself and my need to get high. My morals, convictions, beliefs, and truths had all been traded for a small, tiny white rock.

I inserted the key into the desk, and for a brief moment of clarity, I almost wished that it wouldn't work, but it did. The tumbler moved in a counter clockwise direction and made a muffled click. I felt like James Bond in a 007 spy thriller stealing the secret plans to a plot to rule the world. I knew that I was wrong, but at no time did I think about aborting the mission. I took that money and went on to smoke it all up in a matter of hours. One of my favorite anchors on Sportscenter, Neil Everett, often says, "If some is good, more is better." That is exactly what I went on to do that day. I returned to the scene of the crime not once, twice, or thrice--but I would eventually go into the building an astonishing fifteen times over the weekend. I had come to the revelation that if I could get into Marcia's desk with ease, then I could subsequently get into all the desks.

I started in the engineering department and methodically went from department to department. Some of the desks were locked and needed me to go to the master cache, and others were not. I confiscated everything from loose change to loose dollar bills to items that I could sell at the pawn shop, and since I was taking small items, albeit they did not belong to me, they would never be missed. I knew that I was traveling down the crack superhighway, in the fast lane with no brakes, but this was by far the most despicable thing that I had done to date. I had literally violated hundreds of innocent unsuspecting colleagues in the dark of night with little or no remorse, all for the sake of dope.

As I pulled into the parking lot on Monday, I had the same feeling in my gut that I had back in high school when I got expelled for the drinking incident. I wondered if I should make up a story or should I just let the day play out on its own. Of course, I chose the latter because that is a dope fiend's mentality. My boss at the time was Jeff; we usually began the day drinking coffee and discussing the weekend's events and highlights, which we did and then held an impromptu meeting in my office and prioritized contracts to work on for the upcoming week. I relayed Jeff's wishes to my assistant Louise and we were, as they say, "off and running." The first few hours of my day were spent doing detective work and keeping my nose to the grindstone. I was visiting each department checking on the mood and the atmosphere.

As I approached the different work stations throughout the day, there seemed to be a rush to hush and the conversations seemed to change, but I was hoping that I was just paranoid (again) and mentally anguished because I was responsible for a reprehensible act. In most cases your intuition is usually right, and my psyche was not feeling right. Jeff was paged over the intercom to call the maintenance department. I tried my best to stay away from him but at each interaction with him, he had a terrible look on his face, and if I were to try to describe it now, it would be one of disgust and disappointment. The expression on his face was like a father whose child had ended up in jail or on drugs. And the irony of the situation was, although I was not his child, I was addicted to a sinister and dastardly substance and was on the express train to jail.

As I entered the engineering department, Marcia looked at me in disgust and could barely look at me. They knew. As most were probably instructed not to say anything to me, Marcia could not hide her disdain for the deplorable, disgraceful, and indefensible acts that happened over the weekend. I went to lunch, and when I returned, Jeff was over in the experimental room working on contracts, and when I tried to engage in conversation with him it was not natural at all. Something was bothering him. I managed to stay busy for most of the day and then it happened. I was paged to come to the human resources department immediately. I proceeded to the learn my fate, which I knew by now, was not going to be pleasant for all parties involved, and unlike my other firings, this was no surprise, nor was there going to be any retort.

As I approached the same secretary, Margaret, who had a hand in securing my job, was unable to look me in the eye and simply gestured for me to go and meet my fate. As I entered the what now seemed small office as it was full of a Who's Who of the Unison officials. There was Jeff, Mr. Nielsen, and John P., vice president of production, and the owner of the company, who flew in on his private Gulfstream from Rockford, Illinois for this less than flattering occasion. As I panned the room quickly, my eyes came to rest on the interoffice correspondence envelope that was now empty and a series of desk keys lying next to the screwdriver that I had used to pry open the spare key box and gain access to the crime tools. The executives all had dumbfounded yet intense expressions on their faces in anticipation of what my defense would be.

Mr. Sontag, the owner, would be the only one to speak and he got right to the point. He had the above-mentioned evidence which I thought was circumstantial and could not be directly traced to me, but he then produced the smoking gun. He had Paul from maintenance enter on cue as I tried to deny my evils; he produced a computer-generated log of all my entries as well as exits from the building over the weekend. His report was as thick as a small town's phonebook as I looked in amazement at the incriminating document. My comings and goings were recorded with the precision of a Hublot watch. The report showed which door I entered the building through and which door I left through. How much time I spent in the building and what was most surprising, even to me, was the frequency of my movements. I came and stole over that weekend no fewer than thirty times.

Before I could open my mouth and dig this hole any deeper, Mr. Sontag helped me out by simply saying in a soft, almost caring whisper, "Why, Richard? What would make you steal from a dead man, your friends and family, and put your career at risk? What?"

"Drugs," was my answer, "crack cocaine to be exact."

Although the crack epidemic was not new to the American people, it still hadn't spilled over into suburbia and affected middle-class America and the rich. It was still deemed a problem regulated to the hoods, ghettos, and lower socioeconomic climates. Crack was not in its infancy stage; it was just that the baby hadn't gone to school yet. Mr. Sontag ran over a short list of my accomplishments and explained without reservation that the only reason that I was not leaving there today in handcuffs was because of my abilities and what I had done for the company. He presented me with a series of checks ranging from my 401k to my severance and explained that what I stole had been deducted directly from my wages. He told me to please get some help and that he could not imagine or want to partake in anything that would cause a man to behave in such a manner. All the faces in that room had a look of shock, demoralization, and "how could we have not known" written across them.

Mr. Pillman, a short well-dressed man with a receding hairline had the dubious honor of walking me to my office to retrieve my personal effects. I took down my banners of my beloved Washington Redskins and Miami Hurricanes and put them in the discarded copy paper box that was already in place on my desk. I looked at Courtney's smiling face in a glossy 8x10, posing in a black checkered dress with a magenta bow next to a white stool with a shiny red apple in her hand and thought, *what a sorry daddy you have for a father.* There was no time for sentiment as Mr. Pillman tapped his watch in a gesture of hurriedness. I dumped the rest of my things into the box and he escorted me to the side entrance of the building. Ironically, this was the first door that I had ever entered the building through, and now it was my last. The final irony came when he asked for my security card and key to my desk, the two instruments that I had used to ultimately seal my fate at what I still consider the best job that I ever had.

CHAPTER 7
Gone Slap Crazy

I hopped into my car and immediately started to tear into the envelopes that concealed the severance checks. There were close to $10,000 in payments with my name on them. My addiction once again reared its ugly head, and my thoughts turned to getting high, wondering why I hadn't been fired sooner. My stomach started to get queasy, like I was about to defecate in my britches. I began to fart uncontrollably and I was nauseous just at the mere notion that I would be smoking lovely in a matter of minutes. This is a common occurrence that the addict experiences when he or she can sense the euphoria that is about to take place. I pulled into the bank with a sense of pride and joy that I had such a large sum of money at my disposal. Suddenly, the events of the days past were all but a fading memory. My only thoughts were of how much dope I would buy and with whom will I share it and where I would consume it. The anxiety of what was about to happen was building up so in my body that I literally thought that I was going to explode. My bowels were about to burst at the seams and the pressure to keep from losing control of them was unbearable, but I knew if I could just hold on for a few minutes that all my troubles would soon disappear--or so I thought.

I had every intention of doing the right things with most of the money--catch up on bills, pay rent, buy some food, get brakes for my car, and put the rest up for a rainy day. Conventional wisdom would have said to just deposit the balance of the money, but unfortunately to be an addict is to think irrationally--and more importantly a doper knows him or herself and knows that the easier it is to have access to funds via an ATM or cash is not a good thing. I battled with my brain, always losing, and the justification for this strategy was if I kept most of the money in check form, I would have to make two moves to access funds. I merged onto 95 north from Baymeadows and accelerated into traffic on my way to paradise. My plans changed with each increase of the speedometer. Where to get the dope? How much to get? Where should I go? Who was going to see me? Smoke solo or get a trick?

I ended up in the Moncrief and Myrtle sector and to my chagrin found that since it was still early in the day, there were limited "salesmen" lurking the streets. I cruised the back alleys and side streets looking for my poison. My bowels were now leaking and a cleanup was in order, but not the first order--that task was still to find some dope. I came along one of my pushers and he stated that although he was out, he could take me to one of his "boys" and that he was "straight." In this game, when someone is offering you a helping hand, what they are truly doing is helping themselves by virtue of your dumbness and desperation. Ultimately I scored a handful of "stones" and continued on 95 to Broward Road, which is just north of the Trout River Bridge, about equidistant between downtown and the airport. I checked into what used to be a nice hotel but was now in decline due to what I was about to go do inside their establishment.

The guilt and shame of what had taken place at the plant was a distant memory as I pulled the first draw of smoke on the "glass penis," the pipe used to smoke the stuff. I drew the blinds as the paranoia ensued, and smoked dope over the next week. My comings and goings were sparse but as I made numerous trips to go "re-up," which meant to replenish, my secret was out and with a little help from my friends, I went through that money like a football team through a homecoming banner.

As I emerged from my self-induced coma, which meant that I was now broke and had no means to obtain any more crack, I pondered my next move. I ended up staying at my parents' house to gain some sympathy, love, and the weight that I had lost on my marathon at the Days Inn. Of course, the reason I gave them for not being gainfully employed was a 100% lie. It had become easy to lie to anyone, even my mother and father--, in fact I found that I was lying more than I was telling the truth. I began going to the Day Labor employment agencies, often known as "rent-a-drunk" but that would have been too good to me. These jobs ranged from holding the street signs that swivel between "stop' and "go" during road construction to construction clean- up. These jobs were meant for unskilled, unmotivated, uninspired laborers--no need to think, train, or submit ideas. The company paid you after each shift which was usually the minimum wage. It would not have mattered if it were $40 an hour because all of my money was now supplementing my rampant pursuit to get high.

I was now driving a powder-blue Nissan Stanza four-door sedan. Luckily I had purchased it before my exodus from Unison. Having a car in the day labor arena was a plus, because it meant that I was not as restricted to jobs that were only close to the bus lines, and it also meant that I could carry other workers with me and make more money by sharing in the gasoline expense. It was a horrible way to live from hand to mouth, not knowing if I would have an assignment from one day to the next, and smoking up the little money that took eight long hard-working hours, minutes after receiving it. I was a slave to the man and an even bigger slave to crack. My usage was at an all-time high. I lived and breathed each waking and sometimes sleeping moment of the day for a hit. I started to do unimaginable things to acquire it. I borrowed from unsuspecting friends who had not seen me in years, I asked their parents for money, I even had stories for their kids to get money.

My desire for the drug outweighed any risk associated with getting it. I would travel to different parts of the city and do snatch and grabs. A snatch and grab is when several guys approached the vehicle trying to entice you to get their product because it was supposedly superior to the competition--a sort of Farmers' Market mentality except the product to be had was not cucumbers or tomatoes. As the different "vendors" bombarded the car, rushing in to build value and close the sale, I would either snatch or slap a handful of dope out of the unsuspecting salesman's hand and then take off, literally like a thief in the night. On one occasion I recall putting the car in neutral and not drive and the unsuspecting "victim" was able to land a jaw-crushing right cross in the time that it took me to slide the car into gear. He hit me so hard that although I knew that my life was in jeopardy if I did not hightail it out of there, I had to stop in the next block and "shake it off" for a few seconds as I saw him running toward me like a gazelle in my rear view mirror.

There was an incident when I tried to run off with a sole proprietor's dope off Davis Street near the Roosevelt Housing projects, one of the toughest projects in the city. He was very leery of my intentions as I tried to set him up to swindle him, and as I made my move to snatch the dope, he came out of his pocket with a small-caliber handgun and squeezed off a round that traveled in a 45-degree trajectory that narrowly missed my head and lodged itself into my windshield just below my rearview mirror. I somehow mustered a chuckle as I sped off, dazzled by my own brilliance. The thrill of putting my life at stake was somehow becoming addictive as well. I touted myself as a modern-day Robin Hood, robbing from the rich and giving to the criminally insane…me. My car was mechanically challenged as I continued to neglect it, no preventive maintenance; my tires were "Maypops," they may pop at any time. They were so bald that there were more steel belts showing than rubber. I hadn't changed the brake pads since I had the car, and I was now using my parking brake to assist me in stopping, but that did not stop me from attempting my capers, for I had found that it was easier for me to steal than to work hard all day for less than I could steal.

I knew that I was gambling with my life, but my life was

becoming less precious to me and I often wondered if I would be better off dead. Each time I committed another snatch and grab, the paranoia while getting high on my ill-gotten gains was so excruciating that I thought I was losing my mind. I would have moments of clarity and realize that I needed help, but I didn't know where or how to begin as I was sinking deeper into the quicksand of addiction. I found that there were day-labor pools here and I signed up at the beaches office, which was located just off A1A. LaborForce, the name of the employment agency, was an affiliate of the place that I had worked inland, but I found that the jobs at the beach weren't as labor-intensive. They were not any walk on the beach jobs by any stretch of the imagination, but there was indeed a noticeable difference. I was also supplementing my income by stealing and writing more bad checks.

On the third night of my new-found freedom, I was traveling west on Atlantic Boulevard just east of the Intercoastal Waterway. I was looking to turn into one of the projects located just off Mayport Road to attempt a snatch and grab on some of the dealers that were not yet familiar with my car. The entrance to the complex was dimly lit and as it came upon me suddenly, I pulled on the lever to slow down, but my brakes had other ideas and I did not negotiate the turn and slammed into the curb and blew my front tire. Bummer indeed. I was able to limp into the back of the multi-level yellow buildings and plan my next move. I had no spare tire, no money, no hope. I took a small walk through the clearing and found that it led to a wooded area that shielded me from the road. I backed the decrepit car into the thickets and passed out in the backseat. I stayed in my car for the next three days, stealing, pillaging, and finding a way by any means necessary to get high, returning each night to sleep in the vehicle.

At my wits' end, or so I thought at the time, I came to the conclusion that the only way to rid myself of my misery was to take my own life. I was participating in cowardly acts, neglecting my fatherly duties, stealing from unsuspecting citizens, lying incessantly, and living a life that was contrary to my upbringing. I believed, at that moment, that I had sunk too far to ever be raised. My life was the *Titanic* and crack and alcohol were the iceberg. I had hit only the tip and three quarters of it lived underwater hidden to the naked eye and if this is what the results were, I didn't need to see it anymore. I devised a plan of attack. No need to walk out in front of a speeding truck, jump off a building, or put a revolver to my head--all that would be too messy and would make for a horrific funeral. No, I would do this scientifically. I would not waste all of the money that my parents spent sending me to school, I thought. This would be carried out in a manner that was respectful, not messy--and most of all to me, painless.

As night came near, I backed the car as deep into the thicket as possible. Earlier in the day I had procured all the items needed for my final resting place. I stole a pillow from the neighborhood retail store. I would need to be comfortable in my final hours, minutes, and seconds. I snatched a couple of beach towels from two sunbathers at nearby Hanna Park, while they were cooling off in the surf. On the way back to my final resting place, I scammed Jax Liquors out of a fifth of gin. The drink of choice for my last rites was Bombay...it just seemed to have an aura of death about it. The final ingredient, and surely the most vital, was a garden hose swiped out of the yard of a nearby home. This was so important because I had chosen carbon monoxide poisoning as my fate. It was everything that I sought to end my life: it was odorless, colorless, and most of all, painless. My plan was to manufacture carbon monoxide by simply running the engine of the car, attaching the garden hose to the exhaust of the car, and directing the fumes into the inside of the vehicle all while I was passed out from an overindulgence of hard liquor. Neat, clean, cunning, foolproof.

I rigged up my makeshift death chamber and began drinking at a rate that would make the Dow Jones envious. A few minutes before I planned to "lay me down to sleep," I walked to a nearby payphone and called my mother. When she answered the phone, I never said a word, I just listened to her sweet voice over and over again saying the simple word "Hello." It was like music to my ears, a cacophony of sound made by an angel. My angel. My mother. As I hung up the receiver, tears streamed down my face like a broken faucet. I righted myself and headed back to the task at hand. I started the small 4-cylinder engine, and directed the hose into the back passenger's side window. I had to make a few adjustments to have my self-made tomb functioning at the operative level, and soon everything was in place. I finished the bottle and huddled up in the fetal position in the backseat. I wanted to go out of this mean cruel world just as I arrived.

The car began to fill with the noxious gas slowly. It reminded me of an old Batman episode when one of his arch villains had captured him and the Boy Wonder and instead of just doing away with them, they decided on some slow, agonizing, diabolical way of killing the good guys...and inevitably the dynamic duo always made their escape. The smell of the burnt fuel was not pleasant, but hey, not all is fair in love and suicide, as I morbidly joked to myself. I thought of my brothers and our special childhood. I reminded myself of just how lovely Courtney was. I cursed my parents for my ever being born. I apologized for all the loved ones in my life that I didn't have a chance to say goodbye to. Now I lay me down to sleep. I awoke to silence. I was afraid to open my eyes because according to the teachings of the Bible that I had remembered from Henry Gordon AME Church, in hell I was supposed to spend eternity. There was no fire, no heat...as a matter of fact, it was quite cool. I could hear in the distance the harmonizing sound of birds chirping. Was I in heaven? I wanted to see if the streets were paved with gold and honey so I opened my eyes. It seems that during the night, obviously sooner than later, the car ran out of gas, ultimately preserving my life and giving me another chance to right this sinking ship. I exited the vehicle, walked to a nearby store, and stole a victory beer.

Drugs and alcohol had a chokehold on me that had taken me from corporate America to an abandoned car in a very short period of time. Where was I headed, how would I shake this, what would be my destiny? I came to the conclusion that death would be my only option. I constantly had thoughts of suicide in my mind. I removed my Florida license plate from the Nissan, covered it with brush, and took the city bus back into town. It was a cold morning as I walked the streets of the Northside. I was broke, broken, and living on borrowed time. As I contemplated my next move, I wondered aloud how had I ever managed to get myself in this position--any doubt on my living status was now confirmed; I had gone from the penthouse to the outhouse in what I considered record time. I had no money, no food, and the clothing that I was wearing stank. I hadn't had a haircut in weeks and I looked like a horse with a scruffy beard. I was at an unimaginable low. The shame of a promising life gone south weighed on me heavily.

As I passed an apartment complex on Palafox Street, I couldn't help but notice a red two-door Dodge Colt warming up in the parking lot. One notices a lot of things when the world is slowed down to a walk. The leaves on trees are larger than they had ever seemed, the street signs glow and reflect the light off passing cars like the moon shining on a river at night...these were just some of my many observations as I walked for miles. I was drawn close to the car because the tailpipe was spewing exhaust like the smoke from a factory in full production, and I wondered in deep disgust why the car that I had just tried to end it all didn't produce deadly gas at a rate like this one. If it had, I may not have been in this predicament in the first place.

Suddenly, my mind's eye grew dim and a voice in my head urged me to just take that car. Perhaps the Lord had put that car in my midst to take it and go soar with angels. Besides, the person warming it up was inside, warm, preparing to perhaps go to work, and surely their stomach wasn't as empty as mine. I hopped in the driver's door, put the shifter in reverse, and took off in a car that did not belong to me. I had just committed a felony--Grand Theft Auto, to be exact. I proceeded to where most criminals go: a family member; in my case, my parents' home. I was able to tell a quick one to get me a few gas dollars and a drink. I now had transportation and nowhere to go. This was truly a dilemma as the guilt of the larcenous act that I had just perpetrated was weighing heavily on me like an elephant sitting on a kitchen table.

I somehow got the notion to go to a supermarket, where I had planned to kite an old check that I had managed to keep in my jacket for such an occasion. As I reached into my pocket for the chance to use this forged check, I found that not having a shelter over my person for the last few evenings had literally put a damper on my limited personal effects. The gas in the stolen car was low, my belly was even lower, and I needed a drink. All I could think of was to shoplift something to eat and drink. As I approached the entrance I noticed something I had never noticed before. You see, desperation is the mother of all inventions, be they good or evil, and I was desperate with a capital "D."

While I was standing near the trash receptacle, a shopper and I almost collided as she put her receipt from the goods that she had just purchased into the flap located at the top of the can. While hers made it into the garbage, some from previous customers had not been so fortunate. I knelt down and scooped up a few of the white pieces of paper, and what I noticed were these proof of purchases ranged from cigarettes to pantyhose. The light bulb went off--no, it exploded, with the receipts which contained the UPC product code number, the date, and time of the purchase. I literally had little white strips of gold at my disposal. I studied one of the receipts, as inconspicuously as I could without looking suspicious, entered the store, and headed to the item that was on the paper. I grabbed the product, put it in a bag that I had retrieved from the garbage as well, and headed to the returns counter.

A young lady with glasses and a smile listened as I produced the item from the bag, informed her that I had purchased the wrong item and would like to have a refund. She apologized for my inconvenience, scanned my item back into stock, and promptly gave me back the money. I was taken aback at the ease of this caper as I left the store smiling. Shopping was definitely a pleasure today.

I didn't get rich from my scheme, but it gave me the needed resource and confidence to move on to the next episode. My net take from the grocer was less than ten bucks. As easy as the transaction was to pull off, at this rate it would take me hours to accumulate a substantial amount of smoking money, as I would have to drive to different locations throughout the city and spend some of my ill-gotten gains for the essentials such as gas and beer. I decided to work the Regency Square Mall, which is located just east of the river in the Arlington section of town. My mother used to say, "Nothing beats a failure but a try" so I decided that I would just pilfer a large item from the shelf, take it out of the store, and return in the next hour and see how I would make out. I took the items, a Tommy Hilfiger shirt and a pair of Calvin Klein jeans, to the customer service desk, gave a stellar lie worthy of an Academy Award and walked away with over a $150 in cash. As I left the store I even grabbed two gift boxes of Polo cologne to return at a later date.

After that money had gone up in smoke, paranoia set in so badly that I, in my mind, could see cop cars canvassing the streets where the stolen car was parked. In a brief moment of clarity, I willed myself to get in the car and leave the scene of this particular crime. I headed to Daytona; I had always had fun there and no one would be looking for a stolen car in Volusia County. I hit every grocery store that I passed as I drove through St. Johns and Flagler Counties, and even practiced my newfound trade at the finer department stores located in the Daytona Mall. I had never purchased dope in this small transient town, where I looked for all the signs of the drug trade. I did know where the predominantly black college, Bethune Cookman College was located, so I headed in that direction. The school was founded in 1904 by Mary McLeod Bethune; it was then named the Daytona Educational and Industrial Training School. Mrs. Bethune was born in Mayesville, SC, to parents that had been slaves. She was known as "The First Lady of Struggle" because of her commitment to bettering black people and here I was some ninety years later, not a slave to a white slave master, but a slave to a little white rock. I also was using her institution as a "lighthouse" to guide me to where the scourge of society was most likely to be operating their deadly trade.

I made my way to the spot and in no time I was smoking with people that I had never known before. "Crack, bringing people together" was my motto. I had the stolen car parked out front...and as the money leaves, so does the hospitality that is extended to the now broke doper. It is termed being "out of gas" and once your gauge gets too empty, you are no longer welcome, because now you are a liability and the only asset that you had to bring to the table is all of a sudden gone. I was able to swing a deal and buy more time by "renting" the car out to the dope dealer. I gave him the keys for a small cache of rocks and with his promise to return the car in two hours. As time passed I could see that the trusted proprietors of poison had no intention of returning that car--and guess what? I couldn't have cared less. They, in my mind, had just scammed their way into a Grand Theft charge.

I had been up all night getting high; I was oblivious to where I was, where the car was, and what my next move was going to be. And to make matters worse, at some point during our session, the lighter had failed us and we started burning the crack with a candle--a red candle, to be exact--and as the sun rose higher in the sky it revealed a crimson glob of hardened wax down the front of my white shirt. It looked like I had just murdered someone and the brain matter was blown directly onto the front of that shirt. The car that the thugs had "stolen from me" contained everything that I owned in this world. I was in a strange city, with no food, no money, no hope, no change of clothes or sense. I was about as clear-headed as I had been in the last seventy-two hours as I left looking for "my" car. I was angry that they had not kept their word and left me stranded, not ever once thinking of the person that I left stranded in Jacksonville...you know, the owner of the car, the one to whose name it was registered in the State of Florida, the one who saved his hard-earned money for the down payment, the one who went to work every day to pay for it. This lifestyle had completely transformed my way of thinking. It had literally erased my sense of values, love for mankind, and ethics. I was now self-indulgent, narrow-minded, parsimonious, and self-seeking...and these were my good points.

I headed toward the sands of the Most Famous Beach in the World on foot, which was about 10 miles due east. As I passed pedestrians, cyclists, and motorists, I began to notice them looking at me as I used to look at the undesirable people of the world when life was better--with disdain, uneasiness, and most of all fear. I went into a public restroom to take a look at myself to see why I was attracting the aforementioned glances, and as I looked into the mirror, it was apparent why I was getting those looks. As my mother would say, I "looked like something that the cat had dragged in." My hair was un-combed, I was unshaven, I had cold in my eyes, my teeth had begun to yellow, my lips were chapped like I had been walking in the Sahara, my pants were dirty like I had been digging ditches, and the coup de grâce was that hideous shirt that looked 100 times worse in a mirror. I turned the shirt inside out, which wasn't great, but it was better. I washed my face, splashed some water under my now-stinking armpits. My private parts stunk to high heaven as I could smell them through my clothes and when I produced them out to urinate, I had to turn my head to hide from the awful smell of going days without a bath.

I pressed on and finally made it to the "sand" in a few hours. I rested in the back of a New York-style pizza joint and rummaged through the dumpster for something to eat. I was so hungry it seemed like my stomach was touching my back. I found a box of discarded pizza in my hunt for sustenance. I shook the box and it seemed surprisingly full to have been thrown away. I was praying that maybe it was a pie that had been ordered with the wrong toppings and was discarded for no other reason. Regardless, as hungry as I was, it was going to have to be something awfully bad for me not to tear into this pizza like an alligator on a chicken that had wandered too close to his nest. I flipped open the corrugated box only to find that ants had invaded an almost intact pepperoni and cheese pizza. I was about to throw it back in the garbage like a fisherman whose catch was too small to keep, but I was in survival mode so I did what a successful survivalist would do...I scraped away the archaic pismires and had the best pizza of my life. I anticipated getting sick, but that never happened. This was my first experiment with old or outdated food, which I would soon come to the saving knowledge that expiration dates were highly exaggerated.

The sun was now high in the sky, and being exposed to the elements for hours on end was excruciating. I walked the rows and rows of hotels and condominiums looking for something, anything to "come up" with, but to my dismay there was no scam to be had. I was able to steal a pocket calculator from one of the small stores on the route, so I put it in my back pocket and headed back toward the mainland. I crossed over the Intercoastal Waterway and headed west on International Speedway toward Interstate 95. I stopped off at a small pawn shop and tried to pawn the pocket calculator. The clerk looked at me as if I was from Mars trying to get money for such a bizarre item. As I slouched my shoulders and headed toward the door in obvious defeat, the clerk came from behind the counter and handed me a dollar bill. I bought a beer at a tiny convenience store located just across the train tracks on 2nd Avenue and continued on my way. I was running out of ideas, schemes, and hope as I walked into the McDonalds located across from the speedway. It was there that I was able to get a water and a burger, sponsored by a Good Samaritan that I had accosted in the parking lot. There were thousands of people in the area and I came to find out that the Daytona 500 had just concluded.

The things that I had taken for granted for so long were now the things that I longed for. Food, water, shelter, a toothbrush, a shower, clean drawers now seemed as distant as the next planet in our solar system. My plan was to make it to the Interstate and hitch a ride north back home, but as I passed the Shell Gas station I saw an opportunity. At the pumps, a middle-aged man with a Winston Cup Series Starter jacket was filling his tank with gas. I walked past him and said hello and as I looked into the car, the keys were in the ignition. My mind started to devise a hurried plan of action. It was quick and concise. *When he goes in to pay, I am going to drive away with his car.* Every ounce of what little moral fiber that I had left in me was fighting a losing battle with a gargantuan-sized devil in me that pressed me into committing my second felony in as many days. Without even realizing it, I said a quick prayer and moved into action. As the man stepped into the station, I stepped into his car. I prayed that it started and that I had a clear exit path. The first thing that I noticed was the Avis car rental plastic medallion dangling from the ignition. I turned the key and the engine sprang to life. I shifted into drive and tried to accelerate as normally as possible, so as not to bring any unwanted attention to myself. I merged onto International speedway drive and was immediately stopped by a Florida Highway Patrol officer who was posted at that particular intersection for traffic flow. I composed myself and looked in the rearview mirror where I could still see the crime scene. The gentleman still had not come from inside of the store but I was as nervous as a turkey on Thanksgiving.

Moments later the cop waved me through the intersection

and I waved back to him, thanking my stars that I was finally on my way. In minutes, I merged onto I-95 north, heading back to Jacksonville. I took a visual inventory of the car and found it to be a homeless person's dream come true. There was a cooler with beverages, sandwiches, and candy located on the front passenger's side floor. I began combing through the console of the car and found my victim's identification. I don't remember his name, but he was a white male in his forties who lived in Buffalo, NY. He worked for United Airlines and I was now in possession of his plane tickets and work ID. He had a cache of NASCAR and Winston Cup Series memorabilia in the front and back seats. I found ticket stubs from the big race and programs still wrapped in plastic, as well as belt buckles, caps, and even replica winner's trophies. My victim was apparently a racing enthusiast and I was stealing a part of his life away from him. I did recognize this, but the deal had been done and there was no turning back now. I was up to my neck in trouble and remorse was the last thing on my mind.

I tried to remember as much as I could from the old detective shows that I had watched over the years and I started jettisoning things from the car that would instantly inform the authorities that the car was not mine. His ID, his plane tickets, everything that had his name on it ended up spread about the median as I raced toward home. I pulled off the Interstate in St. Augustine and used the smaller Highway 1 as to throw the coppers off my trail because I was sure that by now that the highway patrol had an all-points bulletin out on me and that I was the target of a statewide manhunt. The car was a white Cutlass Ciera with Virginia plates. It had burgundy interior, power seats and windows, and still had the new car smell. I popped the trunk of the car and to my surprise, it was filled with more treasures from the stock car racing world. There were hats, pennants, decals, ribbons, replica trophies, sunglasses, magnets, pencils, pens, and more...all with the NASCAR logo. I pulled into a small mechanic's shop in St. Augustine and offered some of the good old boys there the opportunity of a lifetime to have some genuine racing gear at a once in a lifetime price. I made a quick fifty bucks on just a small amount of my stolen inventory and realized at that moment that I had a small fortune in my possession.

My plan was to keep the car for a few days, ditch it, and move on with life, but a funny thing happened. As much as I tried to avoid cop cars, eventually one would get behind me and not once was I ever pulled over. I guessed the manhunt was over, so for the next few weeks I lived with a new car and I sold racing gear door to door to enable a crack and alcohol binge that was only beginning. I made it to my parents' house and to my surprise my sweet mother said that a man had come by and dropped off something for me. As I went into the back bedroom that was now unoccupied, I could not believe my eyes. All the items that I had left in that first stolen car had been returned without incident to my mom's house-- not by the police or an investigating agency, but by the victim himself. This was a brain-blower to me. How could someone forgive me for doing what I did to him? I passed it off as good fortune, a streak of luck, or happenstance and really surmised that the guy must be crazy.

I finally ran "out of gas" (figuratively, not literally) in Atlantic Beach. It was there that I befriended a man named Allan as I was trying to return a few of the items that I had left back to the retailer that my victim from Upstate New York had purchased them from. With no receipt and no luck, the clerk sent me away empty-handed, highly suspicious of my intentions. Allan and I shared something in common: we were both smokers in need of a hit and a plan to defraud and not be found by our family. It was the perfect match, Butch Cassidy and the Sundance Kid, Lone Ranger and Tonto, Dumb and Dumber, The Dynamic Dimwits.

Allan was only a few years my senior, although he looked decades older. He had been doing what he was doing for quite some time now and it showed in the gray in his beard, the wrinkles in his face, and even in the sound of his voice. I could easily tell that he was not as educated as I was, so I took command of this ship like Captain Kirk of the Starship Enterprise. Allan, however, did convince me to abandon my futile attempts to sell off the last of my take from the rental and start thinking bigger. His first request was quite simple--he wanted me to take him into town so he could pay his mortgage and in return, we could smoke a few rocks. Bet. It came to pass that good old Al and his wife had just received their income tax return and he had money not only in his pocket, but also in the bank. His wife had trusted him to take care of the family business, which was a revelation to me, because I knew that no one that knew me at the time would have entrusted me with anything.

I introduced him to a female dealer named Laquita, who was young, crafty, shifty and all about the dollar bill. After seeing the hundreds of dollars that Allan was stacking, and the "new car," she cleaned out a back room of her small but neat duplex located off Boulevard in the Brentwood section of town. Brentwood, like so many other neighborhoods in the black community, was in decline due to the presence of drugs, other criminal activity, and people who looked and acted like me. After WWII this neighborhood was a great place to raise a family, for lower-middle-class citizens. It was comprised of the working class that wanted to make a difference for the generations to come by affording them the education that was not available to them due to hatred, divisiveness, and lack of income. Now, here I stood on the wrong end of the pendulum, swinging the weight in the wrong direction, adding to the decay of the very society that my parents worked so hard for me to improve. I was failing miserably at the game of life.

The routine was simple, each morning I would taxi Allan to the bank, he would withdraw money, and we would smoke crack all day. It became apparent that he shared a joint account with his wife and as the balance decreased each day we both were sadly anticipating the day that she would get wise to what was going on and close the account or block our access to funds, but day after day the charade continued. The only thing that got in our way was "nosy" tellers who were getting suspicious of the many withdrawals. One even tried to block him from getting the funds one morning by asking, "Where's your wife, and does she know what you are doing?" I quickly intervened and reminded her of her duties and how a joint account works. She relented and reluctantly approved the transaction, but it was because of this particular interaction that we decided to go to different branches each day while we milked this cash cow dry. There was seldom a time when we were coherent, but in a brief moment of clarity we made a pact and decided that today would be our last day of reckoning. Allan and his wife's income tax return was well over seven grand and we had managed to smoke all but a few hundred dollars in a very short period of time, and the only thing that we had to show for our efforts was a loss of maybe ten pounds each and a big bag of Lay's Barbeque Potato chips in the trunk.

We made a sizeable withdrawal, somewhere in the neighborhood of $450, and headed to Palatka, Florida. It is located in Putnam county which is about an hour's drive south of Jacksonville. It hugs the St. Johns River and is known for its blue crab festival, potato farming, and fern industry. We had the admirable idea of working on the fern farms and earning enough money to pay his wife back before we were prosecuted. That was the plan. The reality was we were strung out on crack, hadn't had a bath in a week, and wanted more dope. We checked into a small motel off of US 17--the kind found in every small American city with the flashing neon sign that reads vacancy and with the flip of a switch the innkeeper can turn on the "no" part of the message to keep you from wasting your time or theirs. I insisted that we never park the car in front of the door because his wife might be hot on our trail, but in my mind I meant police. I had never told him that the car was as hot as a pizza oven, but I had made up in my mind that if we were ever caught, I would take the rap. There is honor among thieves, I guess.

We began frequenting the East side of Palatka to buy our precious commodity. The scene was as far removed from the inner city as one could get but the backdrop was the same: young boys hanging out smoking weed, pants hanging down their derriere, exposing their, as my mother would say, "stank draws," drinking forties, and loud vulgar rap music playing at rather high volume. We made over ten trips to this place to score, and each time they saw that Cutlass turn the corner they all clamored for our business, bum rushing the car with extended hands filled with our new best friend. The competition to sell to us got so fierce at times that it would spurn jealousy amongst the gangsters toward the one who closed the deal. It reminded me of the traders on the floor of the stock market in New York.

On this particular day we received, unbeknownst to us, very hard compacted powdered cocaine disguised as rock cocaine. And yes, readers, there is a huge difference between the two and the one that made the huge difference to us at the time was powdered cocaine--or dust, as it is sometimes called--is not in a smokeable form. This was a pivotal point in our journey because we had used almost all the money on this purchase and a branch of his bank was not located in this rural destination. In other words, the schemer had been schemed. I was furious and vowed to get even with them "jits" for trying a city boy with this masquerade. I told Allan to give me all the one-dollar bills that he had left in his pocket. He could see the rage in my eyes and he could sense that I was coordinating, as they say on the streets, "a get back." I fashioned the fifteen or so "George Washington's" into a knot big enough to choke a horse and had Allan stay in the room as I prepared to go match wits with these grade-school dropouts. The outsmarting was going to be the easy part; the nerves to do what I had planned was another deal entirely.

I slowly turned the Oldsmobile down the same gravel road that we had driven so many times in the past few days, and as I expected the curtains were drawn on the stage of Dope-Selling 101. My deepest concern was gunplay, although in my observations of past purchases, I had never seen evidence of a pistol, so I was banking that my reconnaissance was accurate. I calmed myself as the car slowed to a crawl and then a stop. I checked my rearview and side mirrors to make sure that my getaway would not be obstructed. I played the usual "I'm looking for the hook up godfather deal" because I am about to leave town deal. I pulled out the "Boston Bank Roll," usually depicted by a $100 billed wrapped by a lot of one-dollar bills to back my claims. I told them that it was $200 in my hand and those nitwits went crazy. I had the dope in hand as I transferred the currency to the sucker's mitt, and I calmly pulled off looking in my mirror the whole time. Not until some ten seconds later did I see the chump flailing his arms as he was making an attempt to run me down. I laughed to myself at how easy that was and the sense of gratification that I felt was overwhelming.

I made it back to the room to a hero's welcome as I brashly and arrogantly deposited the fruits of my labor onto the bureau located in front of the mirror in our tiny room. I had managed to take a few whore baths, but Allan hadn't attempted to bathe since I met him and he smelled like an ox. I complained and suggested that he take this opportunity to spruce up a bit, but it fell on deaf ears. As we smoked our ill-gotten bounty, Allan reminded me that those punks were going to come gunning for us and that it would be wise to get out of Dodge. The lack of food, the lack of sleep, the lack of air, the lack of normalcy, the lack of decency, the lack of morals, the lack of being were all weighing on me like an elephant sitting on an ant's chest. I was so paranoid I started seeing eyes in the air conditioning vents--I peeked out the window and saw eyes in the trees, and I could hear those guys talking outside our door planning to kill us. I was about as paranoid as one could get. I realized I was dying from within.

We gathered all of our possessions--which equated to our smoking paraphernalia--and ducked to the car like a Navy SEAL team practicing night operations. We headed south through Crescent City on US 17 south and headed back to Daytona. Allan smoked on the pipe as I nervously drove the getaway vehicle. In a moment of déjà vu, I found myself driving past the place where I had stolen the Cutlass. We smoked until the wee hours of the morning and left, headed for Orlando. The plan was to pick oranges until we raised enough money to pay back his wife and return to Jacksonville.

I merged onto I-4 west in a barrage of fog, not only in my head from lack of sleep and food, but also literal fog on the Interstate. As I crossed over the St. Johns River bridge in Seminole County, I could drive safely no more. My eyes were burning from lack of sleep, my depth perception was drastically thrown off by days of drinking and drugging, my mind was functioning like a computer with an outdated Pentium processor due to lack of nutrition, and my conscience was eating away at me like buzzards on a road kill as I replayed what my life had taken a turn to. I kept singing the song "Renegade" by Styx over and over in my head. This classic rock tune written by Tommy Shaw is a first-person narrative of an outlaw, captured for a bounty, who recognizes that he is about to be executed for his criminal activities. The part that kept hitting the replay button in my brain was "the gig is up, the news is out they finally found me. The renegade who had it made retrieved for a bounty. Never more to go astray this will be the end today of the wanted man."

I could drive no farther, so I exited the freeway and found myself in the small town of Sanford, Florida about thirty minutes east of Orlando. In a desperate attempt to get some sleep I maneuvered the car between two tractor trailers in the parking lot of the Quality Inn. Allan took the front seat and I took the back as we briefly discussed life in the next 24 hours. Sensing that our time together was numbered, in a brief moment of honesty, I informed him that the car that we had been in for the last two weeks was stolen, the car that we had been buying dope in was not mine, the car that we had been sitting in at stop lights next to cops was stolen from a Shell gas station in the city that we just left. He thanked me for the warning as we nodded off into the night. I was awoken by Allan shaking me furiously as I heard the rat a tat tat of flashlights tapping in stereo on both passenger and driver windows. Red and blue lights were lighting up the parking lot like fireworks on July 4th. I looked into the officer's eyes, "The gig is up, the news is out, they finally found me" played even louder in my head. After extricating us from the car, they began with the usual questions: "Where are you from," "Where are you going."

I began to lie on cue and things were going quite smoothly--they were friendly yet stern, inquisitive yet polite, excessive yet fair. The song was blaring in my head now, "Oh, mama I can hear you a-crying, you're so scared and all alone, Hangman is coming down from the gallows and I don't have very long." But what was taking them so long to do their duty and arrest us? The car (or plates, I should say), miraculously, were not coming back as a stolen. Not until one of Seminole's finest decided to run the Vehicle Identification Number did we hear the group go "bam" in unison. I let every one of the officers know, with conviction, that Allan had no knowledge of this escapade, and he was not detained as they booked me into the Seminole County Jail, now made famous for the Trayvon Martin case, on Grand Theft Auto, my first felony.

After speaking with my dad, he informed me that I had crossed the line and that there was nothing he could do for me. After a few days of watching the paint dry at the facility, my name was called to go to a bond hearing. I had no idea where I was going, but as I walked by one of the few windows in the John E Polk Correctional Facility, I caught a glimpse of my dad's Sedan Deville in the visitors' parking lot. He and my brother Joe had come to my emotional and physical rescue. I celebrated once I got home by going to a smoke house around the corner from his home. I was eventually put on 1 year of probation in Volusia County, the scene of the crime. There were several conditions to be met while on probation, which included but was not limited to fines, community service, fees, and monthly visits with my probation officer, none of which I met. Renegade.

I applied for a job as an associate at a national shoe retailer. I chose this profession, retail, because it was pretty much the only job that didn't require a background and drug test. Miraculously, I was chosen for the position and I quickly rose up the ranks and became one of the store managers. I excelled in the retail environment and found that I had a genuine love of people and vice versa. I also noticed by working ten-hour days and weekends, that it kept me sober—well, less drunk than I had been when working a nine-to-five. I still had my morning drink or two, but I didn't have as much time for the crack binges. I recall on one busy Saturday, my boss coming up to me and saying, "Man I love what you do for the store, but you have got to stop drinking at lunch!" In my warped mind I took it as a compliment. I was doing quite well by dopehead standards and was even able to find a nice little car to drive to and from work.

As I got more independence with having my own vehicle, I began to slip back to where I once came from. I came home later and later, my paychecks sometimes never made it there with me, and when they did, they would usually be minus hundreds of dollars. I began stealing shoes as a way to make up for the money that I was blowing. I invited all who knew me to come out and get "discounted" shoes for cash. I was good friends with our loss prevention specialist and I knew his schedule as well or even better than mine. Ironically, the store paid bonuses on shoplifters that were apprehended and arrested, and I was one of the best shoe "cops" in the business. I guess it was the old adage, "It takes one to know one." I was always punctual for my shifts and I never missed a day of work, but as I gained more and more confidence in what I was doing, I became the boss that no one wanted to work for. I usually smelled of booze, was inconsiderate, and ruled with an iron fist. After being counseled for several questionable employee interactions, I was finally let go. I was reminded of the old soap opera that my mom used to watch: "Like the sand in an hour glass, so are the days of our lives."

My drinking and drugging was light years away from the

infatuation phase, and what used to be my refuge was now suddenly my prison. Like the hometown band, Lynyrd Skynrd sang in their hit song "Give Me Back My Bullets," "I drank enough whiskey to float a battleship around." My dad was now getting older and his health was failing, he was diagnosed with Alzheimer's disease and even as much as I loved him, admired him and adored him, I couldn't shake the dope, but I was able to comfort him as he lay helpless in an adult assisted living facility. I cried enough tears to fill a water well after every visit because of his condition. The disease had taken my dad, my hero, and broken him down and reduced him to a shell of a man. I would peer into his eyes and tell him that I loved him, all the time knowing in my mind that if he knew the whole truth, he would be ashamed--not of himself, but of me. As kids, Charles and I would always calculate how old Mom and Dad would be at the turn of the century. He never made it and passed away on May 5, 1999.

I now had retail experience so I looked for work in that capacity. After putting in several applications at national shoe retailers in the St. Augustine Outlet Mall and being denied, my quest for employment seemed bleak. Then I answered a small ad in the Times Union Sunday edition that read simply. "Mattress Sales." How hard could it be to sell a mattress? Everyone needs one, and the ad was so small it appeared that this company could not afford print space, so I deduced that they probably wouldn't be "wasting" money on drug testing potential employees. It was there that I met a young, vivacious, charismatic young man named David McDonald. David was the area manager for a company based out of Houston, Texas that specialized in mattresses. David's job was to open new stores in the Jacksonville market and to spearhead their success. I was impressed with his candor, knowledge of sales, and most of all, his confidence. He had a humble swagger and he spoke with authority and conviction. Although many years my junior, he was years ahead of me in maturity.

David and I hit it off and I was hired to sell mattresses. These were not mattresses that I had grown up sleeping on. Most of these beds had price tags over a thousand dollars and some even cost more than that old Nissan Stanza that I had left in the woods after my failed suicide attempt. I was trained exclusively by David and I took to the sales process like a duck to water. The job was an addict's delight. The entire shift usually consisted of just me in the store and I saw on average about 5-6 guests per day and the money was unbelievable. I had somehow managed to scale back the hard dope, but I had ramped up my drinking and was smoking marijuana like it was going out of style to compensate for the watered-down euphoria absent from a crack high. I really wanted to do well and I knew that David had gone out on a limb for me, so expectations were high and I certainly didn't want to disappoint. As usual, I was promoted through the ranks as I impressed upper management. I had found my niche in the retail environment. I had all the tools to excel in a building denoted by its square footage with glass windows under a drop ceiling with endcaps, point of purchase material, a desk, a credit card machine, and a cash register.

The retail industry is fast-paced and sales-driven. I was able to hold my own under pressure, lead by example, increase sales, enthuse my staff, and multi-task effectively all while under the influence of some sort of mind-altering substance. I was eventually afforded an opportunity to manage the Daytona Market consisting of only two stores, no warehouse, no employees--and most of all, no one to watch me. I consulted with David about the promotion and asked for his input on the pros and cons of such a move. David had become a friend and confidant as well as my boss. He was an avid Christian and he was constantly trying to live a life pleasing to God. He was raised by two loving, hard-working parents but he eventually got caught up in the fast paced, fast money, fast women life in Houston. After a near-death experience decided to give his life to Christ.

He would often talk to me about my spirituality and make subtle hints about my goings-on. He attended First Baptist Church of Mandarin. The church was located in the middle-class section of the city known as Mandarin and was pastored by one of my childhood friends, Dr. Gary L. Williams. Gary, as I remembered, was always a good student, something of an athlete, and although he loved fun, he was not part of our drinking or drugging crowd. I was impressed by his service to the Lord, because not only was his church one of the largest churches in Jacksonville, it was one of the most respected for his commitment to community, Christ, and change. I would ask David to say hello to him from time to time and each time David would return and say, "Hey Rich, he says he don't remember you, man." How could he not remember me, Richard Preston? We played ball together, we laughed and joked together, we both grew up off Fairfax. I would use this as an excuse whenever David invited me to a service.

"Those preachers only care about money fortune and fame," I would retort. "He is not worried about my soul, as evidenced by him not remembering me. He has gotten too

high and mighty to receive an ordinary commoner like me."
La da dee, la dee da.

David kept it real with me by warning me that although it would be a great career move and I quote, "You are going to be on an island all by yourself." I accepted the position and moved all my possessions and my baggage, me, to Daytona. Ironically, I would pass by the scene of the car crime, as most criminals do, as I looked to start anew in my new hometown. I took up residence in an old Relax Inn located on South Ridgewood Ave in South Daytona to save money as I looked for an apartment. If you are not familiar with this famous street that runs north and south through the city and parallels Interstate 95 and the Atlantic Ocean, let me fill you in. This stretch of highway is lined with cheap hotels, liquor stores, porn shops, and strip clubs. Pimps, players, and prostitutes are known to walk the street until the wee hours of the morning, and when you read the Metro section of the *Daytona Beach News Journal*, their local paper, a disproportionate amount of crime happens on the drag. I wasn't necessarily where I needed to be, but I was definitely where I wanted to be.

I reported for duty at our International Speedway Drive location ready to take Daytona by storm. I had decided to walk the straight and narrow and only drink and smoke weed so I could concentrate on putting all that was bad behind me and starting a new chapter in my life. I was able to generate and maintain guests with a high level of success and my career flourished. Although I was not completely sober, drinking and smoking weed, I had somehow managed to stop smoking crack without any type of recovery program. I moved from the shadows of Ridgewood Blvd to a beachside property two blocks from the Atlantic Ocean and directly across from our Lady of Lords Catholic Church. I was a regular on the "strip" as I cruised it for prostitutes. My routine was simple: work, liquor store, strip club, trick, in that order. I was balancing this lifestyle like a juggler on a unicycle at a circus. And just like a circus, I never knew what to expect next.

Daytona was much smaller than I had anticipated and I was beginning to miss big-city life. I missed the ability to drive on interstates, I missed being able to go to the other side of town and do dirt, I missed picking up the newspaper and reading about the most recent murder, I missed it all. I truly can't remember the exact reason, but I began smoking the hard stuff again. It appeared to me that I had more control of it and although it was putting a strain on my financial stability it was not taking control of me like it had in the past. My wardrobe lacked the latest fashions, my cupboards became increasingly bare, my bank account suddenly dwindled, and desperation was setting in like the sun as it disappears beneath the horizon. I was constantly making up far-fetched excuses at the beginning of the month as to why my rent was late. My car was so maintenance-deprived it seemed as if every warning gauge on the dashboard was lit and I was driving a submarine from one of the old World War II movies. I began to float my store's deposit until payday using company money--funds with which I was entrusted--to trick, pay bills, and drink. I even used one of the company's delivery trucks to cop some dope.

I was the manager, area manager, and distribution center manager, with seemingly no end to the havoc that I could wreak. I began stealing cash from the petty cash box, and I began selling the company's merchandise out the back door as well. I had friends and family traveling from Jacksonville to get the "hook up" on sleep systems. I was cooking the books and manipulating merchandise as I juggled my illegal enterprise. Eventually, I moved one of my tricks into my place of residence to "help her get back on her feet" when in my mind I had rationalized that why pay for the milk if you can have the cow. We were supposed to have an understanding that this was purely a business association and that I could have my cake whenever I wanted and that she could continue to do her thing and I would in turn receive a percentage of the proceeds. I eventually evicted her in a drunken tirade that ended with her cutting me on my forehead, a scar that still remains to this very day, and ripping my windshield wiper off my car. Good riddance.

My drinking was now at an all-time high ever since selling a bed to a local college student. I was able to sell him a mattress on the "low low" that he would have not have been able to afford otherwise and he expressed his appreciation by inviting me to visit his place of work anytime that he was working and he would surely take care of me. His place of employment was at a liquor store and he kept his word to the letter. Each night after work, I would stop by and he would give me no less than a pint of Crown Royal with the purchase of a single beer. I was now drinking top-shelf Canadian whiskey morning, noon, and night.

My indiscretions at work were getting more severe by the day. I was sensing the company getting suspicious of some of my activities and shrinkage at my warehouse. Shrinkage is a nice term for stealing. I could feel the walls closing in on me from every imaginable angle in my life. Financially my life was in ruins. I had taken out a payday loan and of course was only going to do it once, but now I was caught up in a revolving door of high interest and living payday to payday. Spiritually I was dead. If anyone mentioned God to me, I would counter by asking why would such a loving God allow me to go through this hell and why wasn't He coming to my rescue like I had learned as a Christian. Where was He when I needed Him? I so wanted God to rescue me, but I didn't know how to do anything but drug and drink.

I missed the big city lights of Jacksonville and investigations were starting to uncover but not necessarily prove some things, so I relinquished my title of area manager and moved back in with Courtney and her mom, working as a manager on duty. I lied to them about wanting to be with them more and how I missed them and how things were going to be better and how our lives would improve. In other words, I was getting out of the kitchen before it got too hot.

My car was running ragged. I couldn't remember the last time that I had done any maintenance on it, and that included oil changes. I still hadn't gotten those wipers fixed and relied on a rigged-up system of tying one of my neckties to the arm of the driver's side wiper extending it through the cracked window and as it rained I would gently pull on the fat part of tie, which invariably engaged the motor and the blade would cycle over the window. I couldn't make this up if I tried. As for the driver's side wiper, it was nonexistent. Of course, I garnered stares, laughs, and ridicule with one driver even following me to show his kids that what they thought they saw, they really did see, a grown man using a tie in a rainstorm to wipe his windshield. I was still somehow able to take out a title loan on that old piece of car although I had managed to skip out on my obligations with the payday loan companies in Daytona--and yes I said "companies" with an "s," because I was able to defraud two loan companies at once. My car, starved from years of neglect, eventually blew a motor on Interstate 295 as I traveled to one our Orange Park locations.

I had gotten back into full-force smoking mode and the lies, deceit, and manipulation reined in, for lack of a better word, my life. I had awoken the beast and he returned stronger than ever before. I was back to spending all my paycheck before I got home on payday and coming up with lame excuses as to why, staying out all night smoking in crack houses and stealing from the household. Getting to work was becoming a job in itself and Courtney's mother, was getting tired of the Tom, Dick, and Harry foolery. I came home one night to find all of my belongings soaking in a rain barrel on the side of the house and the locks had been changed and if that wasn't enough to initiate a change in my lifestyle, I was called on the carpet by loss prevention for some of my bookkeeping transgressions during my time in Daytona. My boss, Brad, a tall gentle man with six kids and was a Christian, gave me the choice to either resign or face prosecution for theft. I hastily wrote up a letter of resignation before he changed his mind and the boys in blue showed up, and here I was adding another career opportunity snuffed out by my actions.

I moved back to mother Mary's house. I had become adept at stealing, so my job was to go out each day and make money to fuel an out-of-control crack habit. My reverse buy back scheme was my favorite. I also would go to supermarkets, load up a cart with meats and seafood, and at the right moment just stroll out of the place as I looked over one of those bogus receipts. No store was immune from my cunning, including the liquor store, home goods store, and department stores. I was smoking, and this is no exaggeration, $200 to $400 a day and had no job. I rationalized my stealing in some bizarre kind of Robin Hood theory and justified it by telling myself over and over again that I was robbing from the rich and giving to the poor...poor little ol' me, that is. And, like every crook, I started making mistakes, not thinking things through and getting caught.

I racked up enough petty thefts to keep the judicial system busy for a year. My jail stints started to increase as well. The punishment was in direct proportion to the times that I was apprehended. First arrest was usually time served, second arrest, five days in the county jail, with two days' credit when you are in front of the judge, and the third arrest, according to the judge presiding over the case, wasn't much more, so although punishment if caught was compulsory, it was not commensurate with the deed. I learned more and more street life with each visit to the county. I received emergency food stamps after each incarceration, I obtained healthcare from Shands Hospital with included regular visits to a primary care physician and prescriptions as needed, and I even qualified for a student loan to further my education. But the only education that I was interested in was the street life. It became a challenge to me each and every day to go out and beat the odds, outsmart the honest man, and to make a mockery of civilized society as a whole. I was at the stage in addiction where all hope was lost and my existence was day to day; I had even stopped wondering what was in store for my future, I had no dreams or goals to motivate me to change, and I wondered why God would choose this road for me. I hated God and when people prayed for me or read scriptures I always listened and wanted to believe, but my circumstances just wouldn't let me believe in anything but a rock called crack.

I was using my mom's car in capers unbecoming to a loving son, and my brother J.P. intervened on her behalf to protect her from me. I came up with every excuse imaginable and unimaginable to scam money from the lady that birthed me. My sweet Mary had been diagnosed with dementia and was becoming increasingly forgetful and easy to manipulate. This was truly one of the darkest times in my life because I preyed on my mother like a polar bear on a walrus, at the very time when she needed me most. J.P. knew that I wasn't fit to be looking after my mom but he, I think, was looking for a miracle in me and prayed that I would just snap out of it and become "Wee Wee," my childhood nickname, again. But, like all good crackheads, things were about to become worse than better with every suck of the glass devil's penis in my mouth.

My dad had left my mother with no financial worries. Like most men of his generation, he had prepared for his wife for life after his ascension into heaven. The house that they shared for years had no debt, the crypts at the mausoleum were not only prepaid but were also pre-inscribed with both alpha dates and all that was left to do was to add the omega at the appropriate time. Although my mom had never worked a full-time job that I could remember, she received a nice retirement package from my dad's thirty-seven years of dedicated service to the US Post Office, and of course she was entitled to her monthly Social Security check. I began running through her money like the Snake River runs through the Grand Canyon. My tricks varied from making up lies to just plain stealing it out of her purse. My treachery was not only limited to deceitfulness by me, but I enlisted other players in the game to get even more ill-gotten gains from the woman who unconditionally loved me. I wrote checks from her checkbook to drug dealers and would then in return take that said thug to the bank in her car to cash the forged instruments.

I was now also going in and out of jail on a litany of misdemeanor charges. I was always wary of that probation that I never did from the felony charge of Grand Theft Auto back in Volusia County, but it never reared its ugly head. My arrests were mounting and included petty theft, driving on a suspended license, driving without a license, urinating in public, trespassing, worthless checks, and retail theft which was my modus operandi. On occasions, my nephew Frederick Preston, author of the book, *Do As I Say and Not As I Do,* and the award-winning short film, *Ain't Nothing Funny,* would employ me to help him promote his ideas throughout the country. Stops included exciting cities such as Savannah, Georgia, Charlotte, North Carolina, and my favorite, New Orleans. The Crescent City, as it is sometimes called, hosts the Essence Music Festival. The festival, known as "the party with a purpose," is the largest event celebrating African-American culture and music in the United States.

These events shared with him gave me a respite from my drug life and from me as well, because I was in an environment that was all about business and executing at an extremely high level of sophistication and professionalism. Fred was able to filter through the muck and mire and sift out the talents in me that were shielded like a knight's shining armor. I took great honor in someone giving me an opportunity to have moments of normalcy as our conversations were deep, intellectual, and full of debate. I shone as a salesman in his organization, as I was always a good listener and I had a good command of the English language and I could converse with anyone from the president of a company to the man on the street, which by now was becoming an all-too-familiar occurrence. But, it was on a trip back home from Savannah that Frederick surprised me with a barrage of questions concerning my dreams and aspirations that did not resonate at the time, but would forever be downloaded into the memory banks of my mind.

Was I losing my mind? Was I mental? Was I demonic, possessed or in need of an exorcism? I was exhibiting all the symptoms of a chronic substance abuser and undoubtedly living up to them as well. For the next few years my existence was hell on earth. I was literally smoking myself to death. I was in and out of jail and unable to keep a steady job and constantly stealing from my mother. J.P. was at a crossroads, knowing that I was not fit to run a household yet torn, albeit in disgust, that I could clean, cook, and drive my mother to appointments. I would also use her car while doing my dirt and it became a target as well. I used to take alternative routes to make sure that I didn't happen by a scene of a crime with my mother sitting on the passenger's side. Other suicide missions, as I would call them, were too risky to use her car, so I teamed up with fellow junkies to pull them off. Increasingly this was becoming more the rule than the exception, putting my life in peril, exposing others to danger, exerting all energies chasing and pursuing with reckless abandon the need to smoke dope at any and all costs, only to be so overly suspicious that I could not enjoy the fruits of my labor.

The thrill of the chase was as addictive as the drugs. I was spending every awakening moment calculating my next scheme. They popped into my already cloudy but sharp mind as I walked the streets, passed businesses, read a magazine cover, or watched television. I was a sick man and nothing was off limits in search of my high. I had cooked up a master plan that I used over and over again because of its extremely high success rate. The tactic involved churches, sympathy, helping the helpless, which as I look back in retrospect, was true about the helpless part. It was a simple, yet cunning, and quite brilliant plan if I do say so myself. In addition, I could work from home. I would casually let my fingers do the walking through the yellow pages of the phonebook in the Churches section. I would then categorically call the houses of worship according to the proximity of my home, the ones that I could walk to, and tell them this believable, credible, and solemn story.

"Folks, I am embarrassed to make this call but the need to take care of my family gives me no other choice. Recently, we had a small electrical fire in my utility shed that destroyed my washer and dryer. Thank God no one was injured, but we did incur a limited amount of smoke damage in the house. The Red Cross was wonderful and offered to put us up in a local hotel, but we declined because we thought those resources would best be used in a more dire situation. The one thing we failed to take into consideration as our insurance claim is being processed is the ability to wash our clothes."

I would then ask if they had such a facility that my family could take advantage of, all the time hoping for a negative response to that question. After hearing the no response, I would then shift into Academy Award winning acting and ask for monetary help for "x" number of loads to be washed and dried, money for detergent and bleach and according to how the conversation was going and how much I was in need of a fix, money for a ride to the laundromat. Most churches, based on their doctrine, beliefs, and need to help in the community answered my pseudo prayer without hesitation. There were times when I arrived at said destination that a collection had been taken up for me and the benevolence of the parishioners exceeded my wildest expectations, and then there were times when I would have the gall to mumble "Cheapskates!" under my breath as I left the premises with my devil money. I encountered damning deacons, reluctant receptionists, and praying preachers as I cheated myself of my blessings and their belongings. I was given checks, coins (rolled and unrolled), dollar bills, and gift certificates as this netted several hundred dollars a week. My closing ratio was well over 90% as I branched out of my neighborhood and into the suburbs. The ten percent that I was unable to close was usually due to not being able to talk to the pastor, priest, or reverend directly as the call was intercepted by an overly inquisitive receptionist or a by a representative that had a testimony of their own.

I also found that the larger churches were less prone to just hand over cash, due in part to their accounting and paper trails, but perhaps they were just smarter than I. The dishonorable racket netted me thousands of dollars as I tugged at the heartstrings of my victims. I got so good at duping the believers. The confidence that I projected when I gave my spiel was a testament to just how far down the social ladder I had fallen. There was no remorse or pity, no feelings of shame, regret, or compunction--I was living and breathing to get high. I was even able to double dip at certain churches because as my list shortened I reverted to calling the same place back a second time in hopes of someone different answering and listening to my words of lies.

CHAPTER 8
Tore Up from the Floor Up

The stage was set; I was now the lead actor in a movie that could have been titled anything from *Crusade for Evil* to *The Theater of the Absurd*. My life, to put it mildly, had taken a turn for the worse. I was literally tore up from the floor up. There was nothing good about me anymore. James' and Mary's little boy "Wee Wee" was now a monster. No longer was I able to hide the person that I had become as I walked the streets of the city day and night to fuel a drug habit the size of Shamu. Not only was I acting the part, but I was living it as well. While many of my friends were working, raising families, and preparing for the future, I was going in the opposite direction. Old friends stopped calling on me, my daughter didn't want to be bothered, and my brothers, nephews, and anyone that knew the "new" Richard stayed their distance. I hadn't purchased any clothes in years. I was now living in a vacuum, being sucked in by the evils of the world, caught up in a vortex of a dope world that was pulling me under and drowning me in a sea of me. I was taking care of and advantage of my poor mother all at the same time. A mother's love is unwavering, and she proved it. I wanted her to see me well too, but I didn't know how to shake the elephant that was sitting on my back.

My days consisted of walking in a one- or two-mile radius looking for things to steal, people to hustle, and trying to pick up odd jobs. Crackheads were seen as the cheapest labor that could be found in the neighborhood. We performed all of the menial tasks that Americans hated to do and we did them for little or nothing. We washed cars for pennies on the dollar, we pulled weeds for a beer, we raked leaves for less than workers in a Third World country. We never had the right tools to do the jobs, but it never stopped us from completing tasks. I remember cutting down an oak tree with a bow saw, or the time that I sodded an entire lawn with nothing more than a square shovel and my hands. No gloves, no helmets, no protective eyewear. no pride, just an unquenchable desire to get that next hit. After returning from getting high all morning, I came into the house to find my mom perched on the couch in her usual position, reading the daily news. I went into the den to drink a beer and watch television. There was a rap on the door followed by a white man's voice asking my mother if I was at home. I instinctively looked out the window and much to my chagrin, there stood a policeman in the back yard. My mother came back to tell me what I already knew--the cops were looking for me. I told her to exercise her rights as a homeowner and to deny my presence and whatever you do, do not grant them permission to enter the dwelling.

I scrambled to the back room like a soldier on maneuvers and hid in the closet. I could hear a bevy of policemen surrounding the house as the one in the living room was putting pressure on her to let them in to search. She was relenting at first and it pained my heart to hear her defending a louse. She kept asking over and over again in her sweet, loving voice, "What has he done and why are there so many of you guys--did he kill somebody?"

They broke her down in minutes and I heard the squeaky screen door open and the rush of men entering. I knew that it would be just a matter of seconds before they were upon me, so I finished my beer and hunkered down. As they were going from room to room they were screaming my name, which now sounded worse than fingernails on a chalkboard. They methodically made their way to where I was "hiding" and beat on the door with the force of a small earthquake. As the door flung open, I took an offensive stand and engaged in mortal combat with them. Although they had guns drawn, they did not shoot, but chose to wrestle with me and try to subdue me as I hurled insults, and cussed and fought like a cornered animal.

My mother was right behind them in the fracas, yelling, "Don't treat him like that--what has he done? Oh God, help me!"

I struggled with them from the rear of the house to the front as they tried to calm me down and handcuff me as the leading detective was apologizing for doing this in front of my mom as the other officers held me into an involuntary submission. I was sweating, spitting and swearing at the collection of blue uniformed "devils" that had come for me. As they escorted me out of the house a crowd had gathered and there were enough police cars to escort the president. The blessing in this whole ordeal was that I was not shot, beaten up, or maimed, although my actions could have warrantied more aggression from them up to and ending in deadly force. I sat in the back of the car handcuffed, shoeless, shirtless, and spineless. I must have spouted out at the top of my lungs every cuss word known to man. The officer who transported me was a young black female officer who I berated all the way downtown. I rambled about the plight of the black man, and civil rights, and on and on, but I never once spoke of the hurt that I was bringing to me and my family by behaving like a buffoon. In speaking of the black community, Louis Farrakhan once said, "We are losing our religion, our culture, our God, and many of us, by the way we act, we even lost our minds."

This was the first time that I was transported to an interrogation room instead of directly to jail. I was smart enough to invoke my 5th amendment rights after the detectives showed me incriminating signed documents from both a witness and a dope dealer, of all people, that I had sold some of the merchandise. I was booked for burglary, a third-degree felony, and my bond was $50,000. I was in constant contact with my mother and she was just about to put up her house for bond after my third week of incarceration before all charges were dropped by the complainant. I returned home to my mother's home and continued to wow my family with different ways to destroy my life. I was constantly getting beaten up by one of the street-level guys for owing them money. A tree branch to the back of the skull, a Glock to my forehead, and a lead pipe to the back of my cranium show their marks still today. I was putting myself as well as my mother in danger, so my brothers James and Frederick were so committed to saving my life they did their homework and found a different avenue for me.

Chapter 397 of the Florida Statutes is known as the "Hal S. Marchman Alcohol and Other Drug Service Act of 1993." It provides for the involuntary or voluntary assessment and stabilization of a person allegedly abusing substances like drugs or alcohol, and provides for treatment. A petition for involuntary assessment may be filed when there is a good faith reason to believe an individual is substance impaired and because of that impairment, has lost the power of self-control with respect to substance abuse. At the hearing, I fidgeted in my seat. I was somewhere between wanting help, and self-pity. Why were they doing this to me? Although I knew that I was that bad, I would still ask myself, *Am I that bad?* In front of the judge I acknowledged that I had a problem and agreed to the court's terms.

I was assessed and eventually placed in rehab at River Region Human Services located at Parental Home Road on the south side of town. I knew that this was the best thing for me, but my heart wasn't where my head was at the time. I enjoyed the place because we cohabitated with the girls and there was always female companionship in our self-help groups and it made for a more tolerable sentence. The smell of perfume and body lotions was a welcome change, a stark contrast from my other attempts at sobriety in a male-only facility where you awakened to farts, crotch-scratching, and bad breath. I once again faked my way to the top and projected myself as an intelligent, well-mannered man to be respected around "the house," as we would call it. I led this group and spoke for that group, all the time missing the real reason that I was there. I began each morning's class with a parody on *Game Day*, the popular football show on ESPN starring Tom Jackson and Chris Berman, by being the moderator and asking different members of the "panel" their opinions on current sports issues.

I truly wanted this to work, but I wasn't ready to make the necessary change in my behaviors to ensure success. I hated AA and NA meetings, first of all--they just seemed so beneath me, and I thought all of the speakers and attendees were all liars just like me, so why should I listen to their sob stories? Another thing that was hampering my success was my inability to put in the work that is required for a successful recovery. I wanted a magic pill, sermon, or documentary to restore my sanity. The counselors at River Region were some of the best that I had been around, because not only were they there to instruct, but they too were in recovery and were in various stages of living a clean and sober life. They looked like us and they felt our pain, which was cool.

I was able to put together perhaps a string of thirty days sober before it all went south. I buddied up with a guy named Kevin who wasn't serious about this thing either. He and I talked about doing some drinking, so I devised a plan of action to do just that. I noticed that there were no fences north of the grounds and if we just went through the bushes and crossed Parental Home Road and made our way around the track of Drew Park, a well-known spot here in town for softball games. We could make it to the convenience store and get our drink on and make it back before no one missed us. The plan worked and we were drinking two, three, sometimes four times a week. As Christmas approached I was selected, along with several other model clients, to represent the organization at the annual Seniors Christmas Gala at the Prime Osborne Convention Center. It was a chance for me to get dressed and give back to the community in a humble and gratifying way, a chance to make a small transition back into the mainstream and use some of the tools that I had learned over the last few months. Unfortunately, I really had not practiced a good recovery program and like most things that you don't practice, when it's time to play the game, its usually disastrous.

I was put in charge of collecting the admission fee, and there were hundreds of well- dressed sexagenarians, septuagenarians, octogenarians, nonagenarians, and even one centenarian that made their way to the event to see Santa and Mrs. Claus. They were dressed in everything from tuxedos to red velvet gowns and they arrived in everything from wheelchairs to walkers. As the money box started to fill, so did thoughts in my mind on how to steal some of this money. I tried to blot it out, but I ended up stealing what I thought wouldn't be missed from the night's receipts. On our return to the center we discovered that one of the clients had been caught smoking crack in one of the dorm rooms, an absolute "no-no" in the world of recovery houses. The thought is, if you are going to relapse, then take it to the streets and don't taint the place of hope. I justified my treacherous act by minimizing my situation. They smoked in the house, I only stole from people who wouldn't be needing their money much longer anyway. I was a sick man.

I was granted leave on Christmas Day to spend the holiday with friends and families. I started drinking as soon as I arrived at my mother's house. Russell, who was visiting from Gainesville, took me back to the facility and although he dropped me off at the front entrance I proceeded to walk down the street and purchased more beer. This was so indicative of my struggle. I never knew when to stop—well, I did know, I just didn't know how to stop. If one was too many and one million was not enough, how did I keep from taking that one that I sought after over and over and over again? When I finally made it back to the center, I made a mad dash upstairs and everyone knew my condition immediately. They suggested I stay in bed but like the good drunk that I was, I insisted on continuing the fun. I was called down to the front office to sign in from leave, it was then that I noticed a note laying on the case worker's desk that read, "Richard Preston smells of alcohol." I was then asked a few questions of my activities for the day and released from my commitment.

I headed back to my mom's house and quickly began a terror that was now tenfold. It is said in AA or NA, when you have sober time and then relapse, you awaken a sleeping giant and he returns with a force and fury ten times stronger and meaner than before. As we say here in Duval County, "They ain't never lied." I went on a rampage of stealing, cheating, lying, manipulating (and these were my good points) to score dope. I disappeared one day after stealing my mom's Social Security check, knowing that my brother was going to kill me, and started living, ironically, in a park adjacent to the treatment facility that I was booted out of for my behavior. I lived in that park for weeks, leaving in the morning to go loot and pillage, then returning at night to nestle into the dense foliage that hid me from civilization. Each night I learned something new about survival and I would go steal items to make my situation better.

There were three apartment complexes across the street from my "rain forest" just off Barnes Road next to Southside Junior High School and several more within a mile radius. I used each one as a resource to make it to another day--for example, I would visit the laundry rooms and help myself to clothes left in dryers. I was usually able to find a change of underwear and a clean shirt to keep my appearance nominal. I would take "whore baths" in the nearby shops, restaurants, and grocery stores as unsuspecting clerks spoke to me on a regular basis. I was always careful to rotate the locations so as not to wear out my welcome. I would steal toiletries, food, and beer to sustain myself. For entertainment, I would resort back to my old steal and return game to have a few bucks on me to have a beer in a bar so I could watch Monday Night Football, or the evening news. I also stole newspapers from driveways so I could always be "in the know" on current events. This came in handy with a lot of my scams as I discussed social issues, foreign politics, and local feel-good stories as I set them up to be taken advantage of.

Since a girlfriend or any relationship with the opposite sex was not on my radar, I would buy pornographic magazines and masturbate in the woods. Sometimes on my hunt for clothes in the laundry rooms, I would come across ladies' panties and I would take them with me to add a tangible asset to my Saturday nights under the stars. In many ways, I was dead, lifeless as a toad in a snow storm--I wanted to throw in my life like a bad poker hand. My days now started in the woods and ended in those same woods. I was arrested at another grocer for making a sandwich and drinking a Michelob in the beer aisle of the store. I was sentenced to fifteen days and when I was scheduled to be released, I was held on an indefinite hold for failing to pay child support. I was able to lie to the judge and convince her that I was a good guy who was just down on his luck and that I was turning the corner and all would be well. I was released back into society to prey on the unsuspecting public. As I walked to the south side of Jacksonville, I needed a drink so bad, I searched for liquor bottles in ditches, fields, and construction sites in an effort to satisfy my thirst for alcohol. My motto was "Every bottle has a corner," and when I did find that pot of gold, they usually didn't disappoint, offering me just enough of a fix to keep me going. At this point, it wasn't so much about the buzz of the liquor, but it was more of the taste and smell that I was truly in love with. Through the lens of common sense, this seems as ridiculous as the boogeyman, a pink elephant, or a unicorn, but in my world it was as real as real can get.

I was eligible for food stamps upon my release from jail. During my interview with a case worker, she left me in the room all alone and I helped myself to her credit card which I found in her desk. I left her office located off of Art Museum Drive and headed to a butcher's shop and ordered over $500 dollars' worth of meat under the ruse of planning, of all things, a church picnic. I loaded up a cart and went to the nearest apartment complex to set up shop. In less than an hour, I was able to sell the ribs, chickens, steaks, roasts, and even be-friend a fellow smoker whose apartment I was welcomed into with open arms. Jackson, was a slim, weathered man who looked much older than his years, and talked with a voice box after being shot in the neck. Jackson committed small crimes and I was on the manipulating stroll up and down Beach and Atlantic Boulevard each day.

My preferred scheme in this sector of the city was simply asking for a dollar to catch the bus to work. I didn't get rich, but it funded my drinking and crack smoking. Across the hall from Jackson was a middle-aged female; I was able to finagle my way into her home. It was there that I was able to earn her trust, respect, and affection. She had a car and that would loom big as a viable asset to carry out my capers and would enlarge my target zones. Her name was Wilma, a divorced white female with low self-esteem and living on disability. She wore glasses, was slightly overweight, and was as plain as vanilla ice cream. She was nestled in between eight different residences in what seemed to be Section 8 housing and was the only European in the mix. It was as odd of an arrangement as Jack Klugman and Tony Randall in the *Odd Couple*. There was at least a fifteen-year difference in age, she grew up on the south side of town, she was white, and I was black. She loved to cook homemade comfort food and she seemed to love my company.

Soon I was driving her car and expanding my criminal enterprise to both sides of the bridge. I would steal during the day, get high across the hall at Jackson's place, then stumble "home" to sleep it off. It all came crashing down one rainy night when Jackson and I couldn't "hit a lick" so we decided to fake a robbery and steal Wilma's belongings. We stole her television, VCR, and some antique coins that she had been saving for years. We sold her stuff in the general vicinity and even tried to sell her stuff to some of the neighbors and drug dealers who lived in the complex. We underestimated

Wilma's resolve as she did some investigative work and her inquisitions in the neighborhood pointed the finger at me. I was interviewed by a burglary detective named Kreeger. He was hard on me and told me that although he didn't have enough to arrest me now, he was going to make it a priority to see that I paid for what I had done. I laughed at him as he left and even had the audacity to flip him off as he climbed into his black city-issued Impala and sped away.

The next day I was confronted by one of the dope dealers about the situation and he accused me of calling him a liar, and he and his boys beat me up so bad, I could hardly walk. I suffered lacerations on my head and face and my left eye felt like someone had put a hot iron in it. Wilma stood by during the beating and although she didn't cheer them on, she did nothing to stop it either. I limped down Atlantic Boulevard heading east; the distance that I usually covered in minutes, now took me over an hour. I realized that I was severely hurt, like an animal that just got hit by a car but still had life. I turned right on Art Museum Drive just at the foot of the Hart's Bridge and noticed the old abandoned toll building in the distance. The building had been vacant since tolls were abolished in 1988 by then Mayor Tommy Hazouri.

I made my way to the small rectangular building that, ironically, faced the same expressway that I traveled each day to my prideful days of high school years ago. I was prepared to break into it if I had to, but to my surprise, the door opened and the place was in surprisingly good condition. It was dank and dark, but there was no sign of water damage and there was even a pallet stored in the corner that would eventually become my bed for the next few months. My lacerations and bruises healed normally, but my eye took longer than expected to heal. I walked the streets during the day and lived in my shelter at night. I even got the nerve to call Wilma and she would sometimes cook me something to eat. She found out where I was living and we even dubbed the place "The Condo." But what I didn't know was that she was still in contact with Kreeger and he was building his case on me.

On a crisp, cool morning, Wilma's cunning proved to be better than mine. After calling her, she invited me over for a hot breakfast. I knew that would give me the opportunity to take a hot shower as well, so I jumped on the invitation like a biker on a Harley. As I was finishing my eggs, grits, and bacon, there was a sharp rap on the door and she asked me to answer it for her. It was Kreeger and he was not in a good mood, hitting me with a barrage of questions about the burglary. He slammed her screen door shut as I looked at her in disbelief on how she "set me up." She rocked in her chair and just continued on about how she thought that I was involved and how she was not going to stop until someone paid the price for her loss. This was the first time in my life that my power of persuasion was not only not working, but it wasn't even scratching the surface. Two minutes later Kreeger returned to the small apartment and arrested me on burglary, dealing in stolen property, and theft. Felonies!

I eventually pled guilty to a lesser charge and was put on probation and ordered to pay restitution. Wilma even let me use her car to check in with my probation officer. My probation office was on the Northside of town just west of 1-95 off Dunn Avenue and my officer's name was Jean. Everything was going according to schedule; I had avoided prison, I was back in good graces with Wilma, I had a warm place to lay my head, and I had every intention of carrying out the conditions of my sentence. As a matter of fact, things seemed to be going all too well and my intuition would prove right on this day. Two officers rushed into her office during my interview and arrested me for violation of probation out of Volusia County for the old Grand Theft Auto out of Daytona. Yikes!

CHAPTER 9
Coming In Out of the Rain

This morning began like most of my mornings had in the last two years. I was fiending for a drink and a hit. It was January 27, 2006 my 42nd birthday. Up until this point in my life I had accomplished the unthinkable: I had flunked out of college, gone to jail, became a thief, liar, extortionist, con man, felon, addict, deadbeat dad, in and out of rehabilitation centers, been at the receiving end of lost skirmishes, brawls, donnybrooks, brouhahas, and pier sixers resulting in stitches to the head, leg and even my eye socket, I was now referred to as the baser, the sperm donor instead of father of my child, the boy that messed it all up, and the quitter. I had nothing to show for my 42 years of existence except distant memories of happier times, and recent oblivion of a world that had crashed down on me. On Parliament's *Dr. Funkenstein* album released in 1976 by Casablanca Records, the second track is called "Gamin' on Ya." The chorus reminds the listener, "People keep waiting on a change, they ain't got sense enough to come in out of the rain." I was awaiting the change but I was stuck in a hurricane of webs, lies, and evil. I still cried at night, but never tears of joy or tears from a heartwarming story--they were always from pain.

I hustled a few folks for a birthday beer or two and was smoking by noon. I was able to con my mother into going to the bank to withdraw some money so we could celebrate my birthday. To my astonishment, J.P.'s car was in the driveway as I returned from one of my many trips around the corner to score. As I approached the house, I could tell that something was different about him. He had a look of cockiness about him, like a superstar athlete has when he knows that he is facing a lesser opponent. I walked past him without saying a word and he reciprocated as I went into the den to come down from my high. When I opened my eyes I was surprised to see a uniformed Jacksonville police officer nudging me with her nightstick. I could see my brother down the hall watching the event like a kid at the ringside of a professional wrestling match. She turned the television off, announced herself and in a calm motherly voice politely asked me to leave the premises. With the remote control in hand I nonchalantly pushed the red power button and Sportscenter sprang to life with the voice of Chris Berman announcing a highlight like only he can. The officer stepped in front of the set this time while simultaneously pushing the manual power button as the voice of my favorite sports anchor died once again. This little tug-of-war went on for several minutes until she asked me to rise to my feet and put my arms behind my back.

I boldly told her, "There is no way in hell that I am going to jail on my birthday, so please leave."

My brother was now in the hallway pacing back and forth

like an expectant father in the waiting room, as the female officer made a backup call on the radio strapped to her shoulder. Minutes later two male officers came in, jacked me up by the seat of my pants, and extracted me from my mother's house again. The presence of police was becoming an all-too-familiar scene at 1850 W. 24th Street and even my mother didn't defend me on this arrest--I could see in her face as they led me out the front door that even she was giving up on me. I was charged with trespassing and booked into the county jail again. I had been there so many times I could have booked myself in and saved them the time and effort. I knew that I was facing minimal time and my mind was fast-forwarded to what caper was I going to pull off tomorrow after I was sprung, to get high.

I appeared in court the next morning in front of the Honorable Emmett F. Ferguson III. He, as judges go, seemed to be well-spoken, fair, and reasonable. He was letting family members speak on behalf of their loved ones and I sensed a vibe of compassion from him. I knew with some sweet lies and promises that I would be walking out of there a free man and would be high by 6:00 p.m. at the latest. When my name was called and the judge asked was there anyone here to speak on my behalf, my brother stood up from the back room like a father at a wedding opposing the marriage of his daughter to an undesirable suitor. The judge asked James, "Are you here to speak on behalf of the defendant?" and my brother replied, "No, just the opposite, your honor."

A loud gasp overcame the large courtroom as the bailiffs, accused, lawyers, counselors, court personnel, stenographer, and even the judge sighed in unison at the rare turn of events. Judge Ferguson asked my brother to identify himself and asked how he knew the prisoner. My brother began his statement by saying, "That's just it, your honor. I don't know him anymore. He used to be my brother and now he's just a dope fiend and I am here to ask you to incarcerate him so he can somehow get some help."

An even louder sigh was heard from the courtroom on my brother's opening statement as the drama was unfolding in courtroom J-2. With a puzzled look on his face, the judge rapped his gavel twice on the hardwood desk to restore order in the courtroom, and made a motion to suspend my case until the end. As I watched the proceedings, I was focused on two things. One was how lenient the judge was, and the other was my disdain and hatred for my brother for meddling in my business. With what seemed like all eyes on me, the room emptied a lot faster than I had expected. I again approached the bench as a hush came over the place. My brother picked up where he had left off, giving the judge a quick synopsis of what he was really working with before I ever got a chance to open up my lying mouth and try to sway him in my favor even though a stack of prior arrest jackets said otherwise.

Judge Ferguson looked me in the eyes and asked me if what J.P. was saying was true. I am sure he knew that it was, but asked anyway. As I began to speak, my brother interjected and warned the judge, "He's a talker, your honor."

Everyone in the courtroom laughed. I began to cry and explained to the justice, "Everything my brother is saying is true, but what I have found is that most people who are addicted to drugs and alcohol want to be freed from the addiction's powerful grip as badly as our friends, relatives and loved ones want us off of them."

My brother quickly added, "See what I'm talking about, your honor? I warned you."

Everyone laughed again. I begged the judge to spare me from going to a prison drug diversion program and assured him that I was ready to change if he sentenced me to inpatient treatment. After some careful consideration he agreed with both of us—yes, I needed help, and that it would be most beneficial if it came from outside the wall of a penal institution. He put me on probation, gave me 48 hours to check in with my probation officer and 48 hours after that to be in an impatient rehabilitation center. He told me how my brother must love me to come down to the jail on his day off to help me and he also gave me a stern warning after telling me that he saw something special in me. After commenting on my articulation of the English language, polite manners, and obvious intelligence, he reminded me that if I were to violate the terms and conditions of my probation in any way, shape, or form, he would put out a $100,000 bond on me and when apprehended I would spend a year in the county jail.

I was released later and went back to the scene of the crime to finish my birthday celebration. I was sure that I would be able to talk to one of my old buddies who ran a sober house named The Alumni House located on the eastside of Jacksonville, banked on the left by the St. John's River and so close to Alltel Stadium that you can see the JumboTrons from the courtyard. He refused to let me back in because of my past transgressions and ability to lie at the drop of a hat. This was a shocker because Robert had been a coworker of mine for years and I had even been duped out of a little cash from him when he was still out in the world of addiction. Time was ticking and my plan was not coming together. I was smart enough to check in with my probation officer and once again I lied to her about having found a place to call home for the next year. I called my "Plan B," The Salvation Army's Adult Rehabilitation Center, but they were full and put me on a waiting list with several slots promised before me. The ARC was my second choice because it was more restrictive, not allowing you to work outside of its facility, and was a church, and with that came morning devotion, mandatory meetings, mandatory classes, work therapy, counseling, and church and Vespers on Sunday. I accepted the invitation to be put on the waiting list, thinking all the while that by the time they called me, I would have violated probation and been placed in the slammer.

On January 31, 2006 I received a call from James Lariscy, the intake coordinator at the SA, and was invited to come in today by 4 p.m. My mom was excited, much more than me of course, about the "good" news, and I was able to finagle enough money out of her for a few hits of crack. I smoked that morning up until about noon and with no possessions in tow, kissed my mother, told her that I loved her, and walked south on Fairfax to Kings Road, where I boarded the 52 Beaches bus to satisfy my sentence. I exited the bus about half a mile from the building and went into Food Lion and shoplifted a Steel Gravity 211 Malt Liquor for the walk to the Salvation Army's Adult Rehabilitation Center located at 10900 Beach Blvd. Little did I know this would be my last drink.

I checked into the facility with little or no fanfare--I can go on record as to say that there was nothing different about the way it had gone down some ten times before…no voices being heard in my head, no super sensations in my mind or even the thought that this time was going to be different; I was just going through the motions to stay out of jail. I was put on an elongated restriction of ninety days--the usual is thirty, but because of how many times I had come there and basically wasted their time, effort, and space it would be three months before I was eligible to go down the street to a restaurant, go on a weekend pass, or frolic in the nearby park.

I had observed some of the guys that had been running a successful recovery program and I admired what they had accomplished, because fighting demons is not for the faint of heart. They seemed to have serenity about themselves that I had not experienced since my childhood days and I wanted, as they say in recovery, what they had. I now needed to know how to go about the task at hand. On February 6th, I was given my first Bible that I ever personally owned, it was donated to the SA by the Cinnamon Street Baptist Church, the first page in that Bible is entitled Gift and Award Bible presented to: I printed my name, Richard Preston, on the 7th day of February '06 and confessed that I was a sinner, lost, on my way to hell and in need of a savior. I put my trust in Jesus Christ our Lord and accepted Him as my Lord. I arose each morning at 5 a.m. and began a healthy diet of prayer, scripture reading, recovery reading. I found the morning devotion to be beneficial as it prepared me each day for what the world was going to throw at me because although my situation was better than being homeless, it was still challenging, to say the least. I lived and worked with over a hundred different ideologies, personalities, addictions, and egos in a church, so the suit of armor was needed on a daily basis. The program was a work therapy based program which simply meant that we, the beneficiaries, worked to run the facility and the payoff was the opportunity to free ourselves from whatever addiction haunted us. I worked in the sorting room, hanging clothes that were donated to the SA from all over the city for eight hours a day. There was no pay but each Friday we did receive a small stipend called a grant. The modest grant started at seven dollars a week, increasing by a dollar each week and capping out at twenty-five dollars.

On February 9th, I wrote to Judge Ferguson thanking him for having faith in me and telling him how grateful I was--and more importantly that I was going to prove all of my naysayers wrong and live a life that was pleasing to God. He responded with a personal letter signed by him. I was on cloud nine. On March 9th I started a journal in which I would grade myself on how I handled situations each day. My first entry was *Today started with prayer and scriptures from Proverbs and Psalms. I was off today and I caught up on my sleep. I served Mr. Wilbur today by printing him information on the University of Connecticut. I am in Chapel now and it is a good sermon. I have to go get a haircut. I am in Addiction Anonymous now and it is interesting. I ended the day with a game of spades. All in all, it was a great day with the reward of being sober one more day.*

This was the tool that I chose to use for taking my Daily Moral Inventory (DMI) which I bought into as being one of most valuable assets in recovery. I learned that my attitude is the focal point of DMI, and I needed to approach the changing and renewing of my mind and spirit from a biblical, Jesus

Christ-centered perspective and to be totally transparent. I had pretty much tried everything else, so why not try Jesus was my attitude at this juncture. I also subscribed to the fact without the DMI, I would attain more than behavior modification, which is simply changing the outward actions of a person. This explains why someone can go to prison for months and even years and on the first day of his or her release pick up where they left off on drug and alcohol abuse. I looked good on the outward appearance but my insides were horrible, foul, and rotten like a dressed-up garbage can. The chaplain of the center, Major Richard Strommer, gave a sermon one Sunday morning and in his message he promised us all, "When we allow Jesus Christ to take control of our lives and become Lord of our lives, then the outward appearance of our character becomes, over time, Christ-like. This is because the change is taking place on the inside of us. Then we have an outward expression of an inward change." Jackpot! Eureka! Hallelujah!

This was game-changing information that he shared that morning, but the two words that resonated with me were "over time." Up until this point in my life, I wanted the microwave not the Crock-Pot fix. I wanted what I wanted and I needed it yesterday, I believed that waiting was for the slow of mind, slow at heart, and slow thinkers. I measured my progress daily as I began grading my behavior, as I worked my program. I found it hard to evaluate truthfully if you are working a good program, but what was a better measuring stick was the ability to see if I was cheating the program. Was my behavior marked by the use of deceit to intentionally violate the rules of the program (and there were many, some understandable, some seemingly written just to antagonize)? Was I refusing to cooperate with the daily routine of recovery? This would be characterized as behavior that shows no concern for one's life and frustrating the purpose and efforts of the program.

I began enrolling in courses that were not mandatory for the center's curriculum but vital in my personal relationship with Christ. One such course was *The Purpose-Driven Life*, based on Rick Warren's best seller. The book is a forty-day spiritual journey that answers the question: What on earth am I here for? My sponsor, whom I had sought out for the first time, gave me a copy of that book and told me if I read this book, it would change my life. I was feeling much better about my situation, my chances of success--and more importantly, me. I came to believe that my life was like dormant grass in the winter awaiting the sunshine and rain of the spring so all the loose thatch could be raked out. I began picking up on popular recovery slogans such as "Don't quit before the miracle happens," "Nobody ever found recovery as the result of an intellectual awakening," "Wait until the miracle happens," "It's a simple program for complicated people," and "Willingness is the key." I kept coming across the word serenity and I wanted that--not freedom from the storm, but peace amid the storm.

I continued to write Judge Ferguson about my progress. I made sure that my letters were positive, hopeful, and humble. The return letters from him were moving, caring, and inspirational, all written and signed by him personally. When my restriction was finally lifted and I was able to leave the center on my off days, I chose not to since what I had been doing up to this point was working well for me. I started a small business by offering to iron the guys' shirts on Saturday nights so they could have a clean, crisp, freshly starched shirt for Chapel on Sundays. This was no enterprise by any stretch of the imagination, but it did afford me a chance to once again handle money responsibly. I was taking baby steps and not falling--something that I had not done in decades. I also took note of the rate of recidivism at the center which was at least 90%, not uncommon in the arena of addiction, and in one of my courses we were told that only 3% of us would be successful. I took that to heart, accepted the challenge, and vowed to beat the odds.

When guys would relapse and then be re-admitted after a thirty-day hiatus from the program, I would delve into their minds to find out the cause for the lack of judgment and this is what I found mostly to be their detriment--it was usually a relationship, stopping doing what was working for you, going back to the old neighborhood, thinking that they had learned to manage their usage, or never really working a program at all. So I took notes and made sure to avoid those pitfalls because I had already come to the conclusion, finally, that I was no better than anyone else and that I was a stone-cold crackhead and alcoholic subject to all the shortcomings of one. I was attending AA and NA meetings regularly as per required by the program. I was coming up on four months in the program and my grant each week was approaching the cap at $25 per week. My daughter, who was excelling in school, had not received a child support payment from me in years, so I made a promise with me and God, when I reached the maximum, I would start paying her $10 per week, or 40% of my "salary." I was learning how to be a man all over again, to be responsible, honest, trustworthy, and caring. The focus of this program was not to teach us how not to drink, it was to focus on Jesus.

A pivotal point in my recovery came when I got the news that my Uncle Ernest, my mother's oldest brother, had passed away. His funeral was to be held in Bradenton, Florida and my brother James would arrange for me to attend the homegoing. He was one of my favorite uncles and had even sent me $500 on one of my many visits to jail, to retain an attorney. I decided to go after speaking with the chaplain, who advised me, "The world is going to be out there whether you are sober or not." After the funeral, the repast was held at his home and there were alcoholic beverages being passed around like food at a soup kitchen. I felt uncomfortable enough to ask my brother Russell to take me back to the hotel. He obliged and for the first time in a long time, I was all by myself with money, and nothing to stop me from walking up to the convenience store that I could see out of my window, except air and opportunity.

Usually this is where it all goes horribly wrong--this is where the baffling, cunning, and powerful disease fools me into thinking that I can have just one, where my mind tries to trick me into thinking that one is not too many and a million is enough, but what I had learned and achieved over the months reigned supreme against the enemy and I told myself, "If you do what you always did, you'll get what you always got," "To thine own self be true," and finally, "Let go and let God." I cracked open my Bible, read some scripture and then wrote in my journal. The Lord changed my thoughts from thinking about a drink to enjoying the serenity and respite of being away from 125 guys and spending time with my Master. It was at that moment that I knew that I would never drink again. I felt a tingle in my spine and the renewed since of purpose that I was already feeling since that magical day in courtroom J-23 was amplified on this very day. "Don't leave before the miracle happens" is stressed in every meeting that I attended--and my miracle had just rained down on me. I continued to grow in spirit and the love of Christ because He was doing for me what I could not do for myself and the improvements were tangible and measurable.

I met a young lady who owned a retail business not far from the center. We communicated mostly by email and she was not aware of my situation, so it took me by surprise when she invited me down to her haberdashery to help her move some boxes. When I told her that I would have to catch a bus and it would take me over an hour to go five miles up the street she was perplexed. I, once again, put the tools that I had learned into practice and told her that I was in rehabilitation and was willing to deal with the impending outcome, be it rejection or acceptance. She told me that she would have to think about that one. She sent me a favorable email saying come on down and she said her decision was based on the fact that it was the first time that a man had told her the truth even when he didn't have to. That was huge. I was two for two on executing the tools learned at the program and I longed for more.

The NA promises were coming to fruition. I was amazed--before I was halfway through, I was comprehending the word serenity, I had peace, self-seeking was slipping away, I was intuitively handling situations that used to baffle me, I was on a roll, I was on a winning streak. I had made great strides from the days of drinking vanilla extract, stealing mattresses from my own mother's house to sell to the dope man to put in his "trap," and being shot at while stealing dope, but I was wise enough not to get too excited or overconfident. I had seen the latter thrust many back into the world that I never wanted to go back to--I reiterate; it was just as important for me to analyze the pitfalls as it was for me to keep learning about a successful recovery.

Life at the center was not without its challenges. There were guys there from all walks of life, with enough baggage to fill the cargo hold of a Boeing 747. There were guys who couldn't read or write, and also guys with mental disorders, extensive prison stays, and sexual challenges ranging from molestation to impotence. There were has-beens, wanna-bes, haters, and players, some with axes to grind and some that were just unloved forgotten souls in the cold, cold world that we live in.

As I continued to grow, I was selected to be a mentor in the program. As a mentor, my name was printed on the back of a select group of men's identification badges that entered the center, and when they had a problem or needed to share something they would call on me. It was indeed an honor because it was voted on by staff and it showed me that more than just my counselor was noticing a change in me. The change was mostly character flaws that I was addressing I noticed that I was still able to be me, only happier, even though I was saved now. I had always imagined saved folk as plain, miserable, stoic, serious people who didn't laugh and enjoy themselves. Boy, was I ever wrong. I was cheerful every day, so much that it annoyed Major McIntyre, the man in charge of saving our lives, to the point where he summoned me into his office and commenced to tell me that I wasn't working a "meaningful program" laughing and joking all the time, and he even went on to say that I was on a collision course with relapse. I was not only deeply hurt, but also saddened that a guy who had been doing this so long could be so wrong.

I made an appointment to see the chaplain to express my concerns with an authority figure rather than take them into my own hands like I would have done in years past and messed up what I had worked so hard to achieve. I looked forward to our meeting and wondered what scriptures he would have me read in the Bible to comfort me, what prophetic words of wisdom would he shower down on me in my time of need, or what story would he recant from his younger years to soothe my anxieties. The meeting, to my delight, was short and sweet as the 70-plus-year-old dressed in blue jeans and a short-sleeved button-down plaid shirt, not his usual Navy blue uniform, simply said, "Richard, just prove him wrong." I took that short prophetic phrase and not only used it in that situation, but I have since adopted it as my rallying cry for anything I do in life. I love you, Major Strommer.

On September 6, 2006, I received a letter from Judge Ferguson informing me that if his schedule permits, he would be able to attend my October 1 graduation. It was on its usual official stationery with the Great Seal of the State of Florida * In God We Trust* seal stamped in gold in the upper left corner, and signed personally by him. I wrote my letter of intent to apply for transitional housing upon graduation of the program, the transitional program gave us three months of living in the center after gaining employment outside of the center. In those months I would be asked to pay a small rent as I transitioned back into society. I began my job hunt with confidence and intrepidness as well. I needed an employer to take a chance on a 42-year-old ex-con, with a felony record.

God had gotten me to this point and there was no need to turn my back on Him again, so I just kept praying, and whenever the devil tried to intervene I just laughed and said, "Get thee behind me, Satan." My faith was blind but true and tested repeatedly. I humbled myself and was content with landing a job that was out of my comfort zone and usual salary requirements. I was willing to accept employment at a warehouse, landscaping company, or fast food establishment to prove to the world that I was indeed a changed man. As I filled out applications, employers wanted a contact number, which I didn't have, so I invested in an ATT Go phone, which was a violation of the center's rules. I was definitely going to be as transparent with prospective employers about my situation, but I wanted to do it on my own terms and not have them call a receptionist at the Salvation Army and under the anonymity clause in our contract have that person either confirm or deny that I was a resident. I kept the phone hidden and used it only for that purpose.

One day while riding the bus up to the Regency Square Mall, I just happened to look inside the huge cavernous shell of what used to be a Montgomery Ward department store and noticed that a new furniture store was to open soon. The store was Homeworks Furniture and Mattress. Once I saw the word mattress in the title, I knew that my search for a job was over, I had found my niche; my prayers were beginning to be answered on a consistent basis. I went in and talked with the owner at length and found that he knew very little about selling sleep. The experience that I had was invaluable to him and he offered me a job on the spot. I told him that I wouldn't be available until the beginning of October and he replied, "That's good, because we are not opening until then."

In my final month of the program my focus was on relapse prevention, since I had seen literally hundreds of guys relapse at some point in their recovery, some of whom even failed on the same night that they graduated the program. I purchased *Staying Sober*, a guide to relapse prevention by Gorski and Miller. I worked on things like stabilization, warning sign identification and management, involvement of others, and assessment. I knew God had taken away the taste of drugs and alcohol from my very being, but I was also wise enough to understand that I was not God and it would be up to me to preserve what God had done for me.

As graduation approached, I invited significant people in my life, my mom, brothers, aunt, godmother, nephews, cousins and Judge Ferguson. Where a very high percentage of the men considered graduating the program an end to a long, hard arduous task, I viewed it as just the opposite, the beginning of the first day of the rest of my life. There would be no more random drug tests, no more shuttles taking me to meetings, no more three hots and a cot, no more mandatory anything. It would be just me and a world waiting for me to succumb to devilish temptations--and by God I was going to use every tool at my disposal to win the toughest battle of my life. During the ceremonies, it gave me such honor to be given my certificate of graduation from the same man who doubted me. As I gave a wink and a smile to Major Strommer, I gave a short speech and hugged my mother; it was by far my biggest accomplishment to date.

By God's exceeding grace and mercy, I began my job the very next day. I took to the job like a duck to water and made over $700 in my first week on the sales floor. I managed to save over $3000 in the first few weeks of work and needed to establish a relationship with a bank. Bank of America turned away my money like a baby eating strained beets for the first time, citing my credit history for the turn-down, and this was just for a savings account. This was one of the first lessons that I learned in rehab that came to light--the fact that everything was not going to go as rosy as one would like but the key was, how I was going to react to the adverse situation? Successful people in recovery move on and consider it a life lesson or challenge, and unsuccessful people use it as an excuse to go use.

I moved on with my three stacks and found that many of the financial institutions had similar policies in place. I eventually hit pay dirt with the nice ladies, Mrs. "V" and Susan, of Compass Bank, who treated me with dignity, kindness, and respect. I was taking it slow but I was in need of reliable transportation as the city bus routes were about to change. I went to the DMV and had my records pulled to see what I needed to do to get my driver's license reinstated. I only had some minor infractions on failure to appear traffic summons, three to be exact, totaling only $215.60 which was pocket change to me now. My big hurdle was Vio 322.058 F.S. Support Delq-- this was the code for suspension due to lack of child support payment.

I took the city bus to the downtown terminal and walked a few blocks to the child support building on North Davis Street, expecting the worst and praying for the best. It was here that I found out that I was in arrears for $16,953, my judgement date was 10/20/1993 but my last receipt date was 09/18/2006 and there was a consistent payment of $10 a week since 07/20/2006 totaling $70, and for that reason on Halloween of 2006 I had in my possession an affidavit to reinstate driver's license/privilege and motor vehicle registration in accordance with section 322.058 Florida statutes. On November 8, my next day off, I planned a trip to the clerk of the circuit court and DMV to pay additional fines that I was not aware of and then get my license.

The offices were not on the bus route, so I decided to rent one of the "loaner" bicycles that were available for the beneficiaries at the center. As I headed west on Beach Boulevard, the wind was blowing in an easterly direction at what seemed to be hurricane force. As I pumped and pumped, seemingly getting nowhere my first inclination was to abort this mission and call a cab, but in what I will call a "recovery moment" I replayed the tape in my mind when nothing short of a nuclear holocaust would stop me from getting a hit of crack. I hit the rewind button and remembered walking in the rain with no umbrella, walking ten miles in the dead of summer, scaling my mom's backyard fence and ripping the flesh until I could see the white meat of my leg and instead of getting to an emergency room for stitches, I got high. I peered down at the scar on my leg that I still carry today, shifted the bicycle into a lower gear, and pedaled with all my might. The twenty-minute trip took me over an hour and a half to complete.

After paying a few more fines at the clerk's office and getting all of my D-6 clearances I made my way to the DMV and was awarded a valid Florida's driver's license and on my way home the wind was now at my back and I made it home in fifteen minutes. God was showing me signs of favor for accepting His Word and living a life that was pleasing to Him, and if this was the appetizer, I couldn't wait for the entrée. I would find myself looking at my newfound credentials at various times in my day--when I went to bed, on my bus ride to work, there were even times I would take it into the restroom and read it over and over again. Next to my graduation certificate, it was my most prized possession.

The Salvation Army conducted a car auction once a month for cars that had been donated to the center. The cars would be parked in a huge parking lot in front of the administration building one by one as each was inspected and worked on by a master mechanic, who by the way, was a beneficiary himself. Lamar was a quiet fellow with long flowing hair that was a grey-blond mix and his mustache was jet black; he was a valued commodity at the center working his way up to maintenance of all vehicles in the Salvation Army's fleet as well. I had witnessed eleven such car sell-offs since I had been at the center and I had written in my journal, "When my time comes, I will be getting my first ride from there."

I wanted to make sure that I was ready because one of the less common but very real reasons for relapse was when guys got personal transportation--the percentage of using increased at an alarming rate as well. So, as usual, I sought the advice of Major Strommer. He gave me the go-ahead, and as God would have it, Lamar parked a 1990 burgundy four-door

Honda Civic on the lot that caught my eye. It was in need of a paint job on the hood and trunk area, had gold BBS rims on it, and under 100k miles on the odometer. I inquired about its condition to Lamar and he told me that it would indeed be reliable transportation. The auction was three weeks away and I had so much faith now, I wrote down the vehicle identification number on that car and went to the insurance agency located across the street from the center and purchased coverage on the car that was not legally mine--but I knew deep down spiritually that it was.

The day for me to claim my car finally came and I was excited to get the day started. Although I had seen snippets of the auction, I hadn't realized just how many people attended. There were cars parked on both sides of Beach Boulevard, straddling the ditches on either side of the busy street and taking up spaces in the adjacent family store and donations center as well. As the auctioneer began to take bids on cars, I quickly learned the art of bidding and waited my turn. By all accounts and from what I had seen up to this point, I deduced that I could get my dream vehicle for about $500. My car pulled into the chute like a cow going to slaughter and the bidding began. I raised my hand and started the bid at $300 another bidder called out $400. I quickly glanced across the crowd to identify my rival. I recognized him as one of my customers that I had sold a couch to just last week. I went over and we exchanged pleasantries and I told him how I really needed this car, but he didn't relent as he and I pushed the bidding up to $800. As we climbed to $900 dollars my heart sank as to why he was doing this to me, but I was not to be outdone, and when the auctioneer said, "Sold to the man in glasses!" it was surreal.

I went inside to pay for the car and my taxes and as the clerk was telling me that I could not remove the car from the premises until I could show proof of insurance. I did just that and drove my car to work that day and made enough in commissions to cover the difference in the price of the vehicle. I left work that night for the first time in years in a car that belonged to me. "God bless the child that has his own" was a favorite saying of my mother's. That night I went straight home--I was mindful not to get caught up in showing the world my newfound happiness by going back over into my old stomping grounds, which was another common trap that snared a lot of recovering addicts. I continued to make and save money as I worked on improving myself spiritually.

When I was in jail, there used to be a saying on the spades table when you and your partner were in control of the game: "Ain't no fun when the rabbit's got the gun" and I was starting to feel more and more like the rabbit. As I approached one year of sobriety, nine months in the program, and three months of transitional housing, it was time for me to take another leap of faith. I applied for housing at the Gateway Alumni House Independent living facility located on the Eastside of Jacksonville. The buildings were brand new and had all the modern conveniences of apartments located in gated communities that were three times more expensive. They were like a paradox located smack dab in the middle of one of the most desolate neighborhoods in town. With only sixteen units available, the only way to get one is for someone to relapse, and that proved to be what got me in as well.

On my last day at the Salvation Army, the place that I

accredit my reunion with Christ our Savior, the place that allowed me to be whole again, the place that I truly loved, I made the fatal mistake and "slipped"—no, it's not what you're thinking; my "slip" came when I went to take a shower and left my wallet on my bed. The thief took advantage of me dropping my hands for just a second and did to me what I had done to so many for so many years prior to my being saved by grace. My first thought was *Surely they did not take my driver's license--there was no need for that...just my money was missing, right?* The money and the license were gone. I stared down at the plaid comforter where the wallet lay, and cried. I guess God had to show me how it felt, what I had done to others, and to give me one last reminder before He sent me out into the mean streets of Jacksonville. I put on the full armor of God and went and got my license replaced and finished moving my belongings.

I heard that a new mattress company was coming to town and would be setting up shop in the Regency Square Mall. The Mattress Giant was a nationally recognized bedding retailer based out of Dallas and huge in South Florida. Although I was quite successful in furniture, mattresses were my true passion, so I decided to apply for a position. It was here that I would make another meaningful relationship that lasts until this day. David Garland was the district manager imported from South Florida to open up the Jacksonville Market of the Giant. He was a well-dressed man who had a bubbly personality and wore fancy suits, the kind you find in the Steve Harvey collection or at S&K Men's Store. He invited me to join the team, as the company had plans to open up sixteen stores in the Greater Jacksonville area and surrounding counties. Dreams always come in a size too big so we can grow into them is what I had been told. and now I was a believer. Keep traveling steadily along his pathway and in due season He will honor you with every blessing, as Psalms 37:34 reminded me in my morning devotion.

I wanted to continue my practice of honesty by being up front with any prospective employer, and I knew that this was a huge opportunity to grow with a company and have a successful career in something that I truly loved to do, so I solicited Judge Ferguson for a letter of recommendation and he responded on May 3, 2007 with a letter that moved me so much that it is framed in my office at my home and it reads:

I am writing a letter of recommendation for Richard Preston who has applied for a store manager position with your company. I was the presiding Judge for Richard in a trespass case to his mother's house approximately two years ago. Richard, at the time, wanted to change his life of alcohol and drug dependence. He voluntarily wanted me to sentence him to the Adult Rehabilitation Center on Beach Boulevard. It was a one-year commitment. I personally attended his graduation with his entire family (mom, uncles, cousins, and friends). I have personally seen a great turn around in Richard along with his family. I am confident he has put his past addiction behind and would make a good store manager.

Richard had some prior charges a few years ago before I sentenced him to the ARC program. Those charges stem from his old life of alcohol and drug dependence.

After graduating from the ARC program, he has held a job with Homeworks Furniture and mattress as the top sales person. I truly believe he has put his past life behind him and would be a good store manager. I recommend him for the position. Please contact me at 630-2577 if I can answer any questions.

I began training on May 14 and I could not have felt better about myself, and I thanked God each and every morning by continuing my daily devotion and critiquing my behavior from day to day. There were three of us in training and I was the only one with experience in the field, so I was careful not to brag, boast, or try to be a "one-upper" or a "Mr. Know It All." I was one hundred percent humbled. On the fifth day of a three-week training program, David Garland suddenly appeared and summoned for me to not only step out of the classroom and to bring anything that belonged to the Mattress Giant with me. He told me that I was fired because my background check had returned and I was not eligible to be hired by his company. To say that this took me totally by surprise would not be true, because my past life had been dastardly and downright sinister at times, so it was always in the back of my mind when it came to background checks. David told me that I would be receiving the Employment Background reporting package in the mail and if there was anything that I wanted to dispute I could and the way to go about it was this and that.

I cut him off in midstream, looked him straight in the eyes and in my most sincere voice and said, with all of the conviction that I could muster, "There is nothing to dispute. All of that is true. I am now a changed man, a sinner saved by grace." I got even closer to him as I explained to him that I was a recovering addict with now over a year of sobriety.

I was willing to accept the consequences of my past

indiscretions until he asked me, "Why didn't you mention that in your resume?"

"Well, I thought the letter from the judge was enough," was my answer as the look on his face got even more confused.

"Wait, they don't have the letter!" He asked me if I had a copy of it to forward to corporate so I plucked it out of my briefcase faster than a Nolan Ryan fastball. At this point, I had to avoid "voided" faith because my faith had been certified by God as was preached in a memorable sermon by my current pastor, Dr. Gary L. Williams Sr. Mind you, I had not heard that message yet, but I kept the faith because faith had gotten me to this point in my newfound happiness. I cried all the way home and I noticed that I never asked God why. In between the tears and sighs, I kept saying over and over, "God, let Thy will be done." It had been told to me in several of the courses to be prepared and to realize that just because you are sober does not mean that you will now be immune to heartache, pain, and misery--to the contrary, you must expect troubling times in the kingdom and the mark of a true Christian is how you respond when those turbulent times come a calling. The need to drink or drug never materialized, which was great, so I went home and prayed.

The next day I received a phone call from Tammy Anderson from our corporate headquarters asking me to personally fax over the letter from Judge Ferguson. I scurried over to the closest Office Depot and sent the facsimile to (972)770-0226 which was two pages including the cover page with a big bold, **"To: Tammy Thank You!!"** in the message space. I received the transmission verification report at 12:05 est. on May 22, 2007. I still have it today and most importantly I still remember it like it was today. She called a couple of hours later to inform me that the vice president of personnel and the executive team would be convening to take a look at my case and after couple of seconds of silence, she spoke in a confiding voice as she said to me, "Richard, I am not supposed to say this to you, but if I were you, I wouldn't worry" as she wished me a blessed day and hung up!

I opened up my Bible to Psalms 19:7. *The Law of the Lord is perfect. Converting the soul: The testimony of the Lord is sure, making wise the simple.* My journal entry for the day was: *"Today was spent talking and faxing and emailing the letter from Judge Ferguson to corporate headquarters, I am being reviewed and things seem to be more positive than negative. They are going to call me tomorrow. I am praying for good news.* This is my entry on 05/23, *Doing the deal and having faith came back in my favor. I love this. I am now an official employee of Mattress Giant. I spoke at the Salvation Army.*

David Garland welcomed me back to training with open arms and I looked him deep into his eyes, shook his hand as firmly as I could without breaking it and made the sincerest promise that I had ever made to anyone in my life: "You will never regret what you just did for me." I returned to the training class and either caught the ire or the admiration of my fellow trainees with one being totally against my return and the other, as I would later find out, feeling the same way but was more of a professional and kept his feelings to himself. I was careful to stay humble in training as I graduated as the top trainee. I quickly rose to top salesman and promoted to store manager of a brand new store in the Baymeadows area of Jacksonville. I moved out of the Alumni House in good standing and began taking care of my mother, who was now suffering from dementia and diabetes. I cooked, made sure she had her medications, and reminisced with her on a daily basis. I had her house painted, screens replaced, and a laid a beautiful lawn with plenty of plants and flowers for her to water to her heart's content.

The Mattress Giant was growing in leaps and bounds as we all jockeyed for higher- volume stores. One such prize was the highly anticipated opening of our Palm Coast store in Flagler County, about an hour south of Jacksonville. Bob was slated to be the manager of that store as he had dutifully traveled here while his store was under construction. As the store was about to open, I received an unexpected call from David Garland, asking me to help open the location as Bob had been deemed unable to work alone. "Of course" was my response, as I wondered to myself as to the real reason for the sudden change in personnel. Then, about an hour later, the call was much more frantic as David offered me the store manager position. I told him that I would have to think about that, since I had taken on the responsibility of taking care of my mom and it also conjured up bad times in Daytona. When I called him back, I still hadn't made a decision, and I asked him for more time. I could tell in his voice that he needed me and I remembered the pledge that I had made to him.

It was a no-brainer, but before I gave him my final decision, my inquiring mind had to ask, "What happened to Bob?" Well, it seemed that Bob was inebriated at work and made an unwanted sexual advance to a female contractor and when David went over to the store to speak to him about it, Bob was caught off guard and accidentally spilled his adult beverage all over the desk. In one of the most God-conceived and power-sustaining guiding events of human destiny, some might call it karma, he put me in a position to elevate my newfound sobriety, giving me testimony after testimony to be a living example and to show the world His sufficient grace and mercy and to help others suffering from similar maladies. Instead of uprooting and moving to Palm Coast, I would just put the Civic on the road each day and handle my business. I was offered a nice compensation package and mileage.

The store turned out to be better than expected and I saw my income increase from about 45k to over 70k. The Civic was reliable transportation as I traveled close to 150 miles per day. My brother used to tease me that the tires and rims were worth more than the car. The AC finally conked out in 2008, and I needed that for the long drive to work in the Florida heat. Gasoline was also at an all-time high, so I decided to get a new fuel-efficient Hyundai Accent or Elantra from a dealership that had funny commercials and was close to my house. What I didn't realize was that because of the soaring fuel costs, efficient cars were expensive and guzzlers were inexpensive, the law of supply and demand. As I walked the lot in shock, I was heading back to the Honda to regroup and rethink this whole new car thing.

As I was about to leave I saw a blue Mercedes that caught my eye so I asked a salesman, "Does that belong to someone who works here, or is it for sale?" It was four years old with 40,000 miles on it and appeared to be in fantastic condition, and was about the same price as the economy cars that I had originally come to buy. I signed on the dotted line on May 1st, 2008, a little over a year after transitioning from the world of rehabilitation. The message that I am trying to convey here is not one of materialism, but one of freedom to do or be what one chooses to when the chains and shackles of addiction are replaced with the fine jewelry of Jesus Christ.

My career steadily increased while my mother's health decreased, so I was able to do special things for her, like bringing her flowers, taking her to fine restaurants, and hiring someone to clean her house. Later that year I was informed that I had been awarded the Giant's Greatest award for being one of the top two salespeople in my district. The coveted award came with an all-expense-paid trip to one of the Caribbean's most luxurious vacation resorts in the world, The Atlantis, located in the Bahamas on Paradise Island. I was cautiously excited as I knew that there were some obstacles ahead of me that would make taking this trip a little more challenging than most. One was who would take care of my mom when I was gone, and two was that I had no passport. To obtain this official document issued by our government that would entitle me to travel under its protection to and from foreign countries, I would need just a few identifying documents that were, if not at my immediate disposal, easily attainable. Armed with my documents as I headed to the United States Post Office, it was with much vexation that I was informed of the need to be current on one's child support before a visa could be issued. A trip to the same child support enforcement office that had just recently enabled me to get a valid driver's license confirmed what I had been told. Under a program called "Passport Denial," authorized by a 1997 amendment to a law called the Personal Responsibility and Work Opportunity Reconciliation Act, any person who owes child support in an amount greater than $2,500 will be denied a US passport.

My child support had ballooned up to about $600 a month as I was now required to pay both the actual support and my arrearages obligation, a commitment that I did not take lightly. I paid each payday with my head held high, now realizing that I had failed my child both financially and spiritually as well, but I still owed in excess of twenty thousand dollars. I kept the faith in God's power to handle all of my situations, but I must confess, it was smaller than the size of a mustard seed on this one. David and I had spoken about the situation and if I wasn't able to secure the passport within a certain date, I would do the honorable thing and defer my prize to the runner-up. The deadline was now a day away so I decided to at least do the possible on my end and give it to God so He could do the impossible. After visiting a private lawyer and the state attorney's office, the one thing they both agreed to was this was a child support enforcement matter and if there was to be a resolution in my favor, that was the place to begin.

I was about to give up and go home because let's just say, the customer experience is not what they are known for, but then the Holy Spirit reminded me to first seek God for direction, submit to Him in all things and draw strength from Him, as I had read in my daily devotional. I quickly changed my direction and my attitude and went to claim what was rightfully mine. I got on the elevator, said a silent prayer, and exited on the appropriate floor. Although the surroundings were the same, the room seemed different. I approached a young lady reading a KMART advertisement and patiently waited for her to look up at me being ever so careful not to startle her. She eventually peered over the double folded color section of what seemed to be the children's clothing section and waited for me to speak first. In Sales 101 you are taught that the first one to speak loses, so I waited until she said, as her neck slid to one side, "Yes?" as she chewed her gum faster.

I took a deep breath because I knew that if I did not "come correct" to her, this chance meeting would be over before it even began. I cleared my throat and as humbly as I could, apologized for interrupting her work. She smiled and soaked it up like a sponge dropped in a bucket of water as I spoke slowly and softly, making sure not to be perceived as a "know-it-all" as I put the ball in her court by saying, "I am not sure that I am in the right place or that you can even help me with my plight?" I started by explaining my job and the contest, then grabbed her attention by having her visualize herself in the Bahamas. One of the most notable character defects for addicts is manipulation, so I was careful to make sure that the conversation was a dialogue, so as not to be manipulative which was a line as fine as a frog's hair that I did not want to cross.

She warmed up to me and after talking for a few minutes she actually looked my name up in the computer system, confirmed that I was in arrears, but unlike my other visits, she motioned for me to go out into a designated spot in the waiting area and someone would be with me shortly. The someone turned out to be a supervisor in the passport department. She was a long thin older lady in a smartly put together grey business suit, who seemed to magically appear out of nowhere and called my name. I followed her through a series of corridors as we made our way through the maze of cubicles before finally coming to rest in a large well-decorated office with a degree and certificates hanging from the wall. There were photos of her family and what seemed to be vacation photos.

We exchanged pleasantries and she seemed more intrigued by my recovery story than my trip to the Caribbean. She conveyed the compassion of a mother and the demeanor of a librarian as she went from screen to screen on her computer. She inched closer to the monitor, positioned her glasses on top of her head and said with extreme enthusiasm and confidence, "Mr. Preston, for some reason, which I do not have the answer, the State of Florida has asked Washington to release your passport."

"So what does that mean exactly?" I asked inquisitively like a child who did not quite understand an answer from his mother.

With tears streaming from the corner of her eyes, she said, "You will be able to make your trip," and she went on to say how she had never seen this happen before and to make me feel even better, implied that it may have been the gallant effort that I made while in rehabilitation, or as she looked around the room to make sure it was for our ears only, God at work in my life. She gave me instructions on what to do next and even supplied me with her personal cell number to help in expediting the document, which would come out of Miami. Two weeks later my visa arrived at my doorstep via Federal Express. Jesus said, "I am the light of the world, he who follows Me shall not walk in darkness, but have the light of life." He sees every weed as a potential rose, every doubter as a potential believer, and every sinner as a potential saint. I won that contest for the next four years in a row.

I met my beautiful wife, Desiree, while I was escorting another woman to my wife's Christmas party. As God would have it, I was seated next to her during dinner and I found myself watching her more than the steak on my plate. I dreamed of her for the next week and devised a plan to call on her. It was with my nephew and my barber's help that I found the location of her office. After an extra-special haircut one Thursday, my barber convinced me to make my move. When I arrived at her office she was not there but her assistant was so mesmerized by my quest for love that she called my wife on the phone and let me talk to her. Desiree was more shy than I had anticipated and was obviously reluctant to accept a dinner date, and rightfully so, due to the fact that the last time she saw me there was another girl in my company. I pressed the issue, she relented and we had our first date at Bonefish Grill in the Mandarin area of town. She had the most beautiful eyes that I had ever seen and I looked into them throughout dinner. I took her back home and kissed her tenderly on the lips. We had several dates as I shared my story with her and she shared hers with me.

I was making headway but not until I invited her to hear me speak at a Narcotics Anonymous meeting did she fall all the way in love. We were married on March 6th, Courtney's birthday, 2010 on the cruise ship *Fascination* by the Honorable Emmett F. Ferguson III. The man who initiated my recovery now cemented my happiness for the rest of my life with a bride sent to me by God. All of my groomsmen were men that I had betrayed, cheated, or scammed in some way shape or form. My brother James, my high school chum Kyle Dean, my nephew Frederick, and my best man was nephew Rodney Preston, my old drinking buddy, who by the way, found the Lord and quit drinking years before me. Nap, who never left me spiritually, but refused to be a part of my foolishness and self-destruction, was there with his lovely wife, Dawn, as well. My godmother Mrs. Almeta was there, and the special guest of honor, dressed in white, escorted by my brother Russell, was my beautiful mother Mary. A combination of pride surrounded by happiness was in the atmosphere at our wedding, and my beautiful bride was as happy as I had ever seen her, eager to share the man whom so many had discarded like last week's trash.

Some things were easier to overcome than others, including my relationship with my daughter. With my newfound financial success, I made mistakes by trying to buy back her trust. I had funded an extravagant seafood bash on her graduation from Paxon Advanced Studies back in 2008. The school was ranked in the top 15 in the nation for academic excellence as she performed admirably in my absence, a testament to her mother. She was accepted into the University of Central Florida located in Orlando and graduated with a degree in criminal justice four years later. She accepted her first position at a Juvenile Detention Center in Key West. It was not until then that the chasm that I had widened so vast in our relationship would take a 180- degree turnaround. She reached out to me for help in the move, a call that I had awaited and prepared for as I let God's hand work His magic. I had learned not to interfere in the God of Salvation's work-- and here comes that word again, to have faith.

In my morning devotional I read that you don't need faith unless you're hoping for something. You can have an *expression* of faith, yet not enjoy the *benefits* of faith. You can get excited about a sermon in church, yet nothing changes in your life. Faith is not an emotion; it's a decision to stand on God's Word. Courtney was requesting her dad's input, guidance, and financial support on her first major decision of her life. I left Jacksonville and was to pick her up from her apartment in the Land of Disney. As much as I was anticipating the ride, I was nervous as well. We would be on the road, locked in the driver's and passenger's seat only feet apart for over eight hours. I had not been in the position to have a one-on-one chit-chat with my daughter for over eight years and I was terrified about what she might ask and even more how I would answer. I arrived about 4:00 in the morning, the first time seeing where she had lived for the past four years. I loaded her small bag into the trunk as she clung to her old "blankey" that I remembered from when she was just a baby. I applauded her for being on time and her response was, "I got it from you." Those words were solace to my inner soul and we spent the next eight hours reminiscing and reacquainting ourselves with one another.

When she pulled her cover over her thin body and finally fell asleep on our long journey, I kept looking at her like a parent does a newborn and thanking God for keeping her until I returned to manhood. In one aspect it was like we had never been apart, and on the other I was amazed by how much she still valued what I had to say--my ideas, visions, hopes, and dreams all seemed relevant to her, and I loved her for the young lady she had become and for forgiving a wretch like me. We conducted our business and procured her a small apartment on the famed Duval Street in downtown Key West, just blocks from Mile Marker One on US Hwy One, had a fabulous dinner, and retired to our rooms for the trek back home in the morning. She called a few minutes later to ask if she could use the car to go to the movies, and in a fatherly tone, I explained about it being late, her safety, and if something did happen how sick I would be after spending such quality time. She agreed and I cried myself to sleep.

Giving back to others with similar transgressions is a part of the recovery process that is stressed and when I was hard questioning guys who were relapsing, this process never occurred so when the chance to speak at NA or AA meetings arose, I jumped at the chance. I eventually volunteered at an organization called The Bridge, a halfway house of sorts for prisoners on the last months of their sentence and housed in a minimal security facility, to facilitate a class on the book that saved my life by Rick Warren, *A Purpose Driven Life*. The class was strictly voluntary and my attendees reminded me of me when I was lost and wasn't sure in which direction to turn. Most were Christians and had the head knowledge but were lacking in the heart knowledge, a major juxtaposition that I see when speaking to recovery groups, but I never judge. I was also still a faithful member of the Salvation Army.

It was my dear wife who proclaimed, "I know that you have an allegiance to the Army and God knows I love them too for what they helped you accomplish, but as husband and wife, we need to find a church and make it our home." She suggested First Baptist Church of Mandarin where my schoolmate Gary L. Williams Sr. was the pastor. I reminded her that I didn't want to go to a "big" church and get lost in the shuffle, not be able to speak with the pastor, and yes, dare I say it, fund an extravagant lifestyle. This was the guy that I had asked several of his parishioners to ask if he remembered me from the neighborhood and Joseph Stilwell Junior High school only to be told, "No, he don't remember you, man." I accepted Desiree's invitation just to go and prove her wrong and me right (obviously I still had some growing to do) and upon entering the church, we turned the corner and as we were making our way to the sanctuary, he noticed me immediately, excused himself from his conversation, and greeted me with open arms and said, "What's up, Richard Preston!"

Desiree looked at me with that look that only a wife can give and together we joined the church in June 2011. I was hungry for God's gifts and the opportunity to redeem myself as a lover of Christ, father, and son, so I was baptized in my new church home a week later. As fate would have it, Nap and his wife were the first couple to be married at the present location and he and the pastor are close friends. Whenever Nap travels to town we all get together and have lunch and share laughs, and that same pastor that I thought would never even take a phone call from me has taken time out his busy schedule to break bread, listen to my story, and pray for a man who one night slept in a tree just to survive.

On one such occasion we were enjoying lunch at the Metro Diner with Nap, the pastor, and our executive pastor, Steve Newbill, who used to work at State Farm Insurance before being called to preach. He learned of my prior years with the company and asked, "So Rich, why did you leave State Farm?" and before I could formulate a politically correct answer, Nap chimed in and said simply, "Because they asked him to." As laughter erupted at the table, I was reminded of what I used to think was fun and what fun I was having now and it reminded me of a quote in one of my morning devotionals when the question is asked: How can you know your spiritual condition? Answer: By the company you keep and the choices you make. When you are free to go, where do you chose to go? Whose company do you prefer?

After dropping the pastors back at the church. my good friend insisted on seeing my mother, who was now in St. Catherine's Adult Living Alzheimer's Unit, as she needed 24-hour care. I remember her smiling when we arrived, and after the visit my good friend and I shared tears and an embrace. My mom passed away on July 23, 2011 and one of the first calls that I received was from that same pastor that I thought would never have time for a nobody like me, and just when I thought the blessings were too much for me to fathom, he showed up unannounced at her funeral. She was laid to rest in the crypt where my father was awaiting her presence in Mausoleum CC-28 in Restlawn Cemetery, a few miles from our house on 24th Street.

After our congregation completed a series called *Living 3D Plus One* making God the priority not just a priority, a course designed by our leader to bring the believer into a richer knowledge of God's purpose, focusing on a deeper commitment to Christ, Church, Community and Change, I was invited to share a portion of my story with the august body of believers at First Church. I was invited back to share my testimony on Watch Night of the same year. As I surveyed the crowd as I spoke, I could see three different types of reactions: some in utter disbelief, many had a confused look, and others seemed to be saying, "I am struggling with something just as powerful in my life at this very moment. "it may not be alcohol, drugs. or suicide but something is pulling me farther and farther from God like space debris caught in the gravitational pull of a distant planet. I explained to the crowd that I had taken so many bites of the apple I had swallowed the core and the only way to heal was to get real. In recovery as well as in life too many of us, just like I did, concentrate too much on the H-O-W...how did I get in this predicament, how did I fail, how is it going to end? These are normal, standard questions that one asks him or herself but the concentration, as preached so eloquently by my Pastor of Operations, Pastor Kevin Smith, should be on the W-H-O, and that answer is Jesus because when I was not concerned about living for Him, He was concerned about living for me. He is the great "I am" and wants to prove to us that the greater the mess, the bigger the miracle.

I currently manage not one but six stores, with the title of Area Manager from the same company that I stole from, lied to, and had no loyalty to. I have not had a drink or drug in over ten years and I have begun my quest to travel the world and spread the saving knowledge of Jesus Christ. In July 2014, I was blessed to be part of our church's mission team that traveled to Malawi, Africa where since 2000 our pastor's vision has led our church to build two educational facilities, a cafeteria and dining hall, teacher's housing and electrical substation and men and women's lavatories. That trip opened my eyes even further to the plight of the human spirit and why God is vital in each and every life on the planet.

As some might call the most powerful nerd in the universe, Neil DeGrasse Tyson, a black astrophysicist, puts it, "Every single event that can happen does happen." They just take place in parallel worlds. It's like an infinite garden of endlessly forking paths. To make sense of this, every time I flip a coin and say heads or tails that is just some little quantum accident. The Universe is splitting into two worlds every time it comes up heads or tails. So, our experience of the splitting is like the experience of walking through a garden of paths that fork and when we come to a fork in the path we take one or the other (heads or tails) and although both exist at the same time, we can only experience one of them."

In one universe there is the choice of not following the word of Jesus and all the consequences that come with that, and in the other, there is the choice of feasting on God's Word and living a life that is pleasing to Him and being promised eternal glory. "Life is a place of endlessly forking paths and parallel realities, a place where every version of every event for every living organism on earth is happening somewhere. The number of possibilities is growing exponentially, doubling every time you flip that coin." I choose not to flip that coin anymore; I choose life and life in more abundance, as promised by my Lord. I choose to use my testimony, my strength, experience, and hope to help change the lives of others and to be a living, breathing example of what God can do. It's true, a tiger can't change his stripes, but a human being can be born again, regenerated, rejuvenated, and excavated from the living dead to become a positive contributor to society. I was my own flame, fuse, and bomb but God never met a man He couldn't save.

It is said that Satan tempts you and God tests you and with that in mind, I have continued to have my morning daily devotional that I began over ten years ago—it's simple, consistent, and effective, starting each morning with prayer and thanking our Father for things I used to take for granted, like oxygen to breathe, keeping me in my slumber, and a warm bed to rest my head. I read a chapter out of the Bible, first the King James Version and then that same chapter from the New International Version. I read from Genesis to Revelation, page by page, chapter by chapter, verse by verse from start to finish. I have been given suggested ways on my reading but I stick to my original way because it works for me and with my rudimentary way of doing so, I have been able to completely read the Holy Scripture in its entirety three times. There are two reasons why I refuse to change--one, it works for me; and two, every time in the past that I have tried to alter God's plan for me, it has gone horribly wrong, so I remove myself from the equation and follow God's command. I also read our church-supplied Daily Devotional, The Word For You Today which I have quoted from several times in this book.

My wife keeps me supplied with other devotionals ranging from Rick Warren to Joel Osteen that I add to my repertoire and I end just like I began when I got saved in 2006. I make an entry in my journal, asking God for the pardon of my sins, and jotting down where I missed the mark on the previous day, areas of opportunity for growth, thanking Him for good days and bad days alike, putting Him first, and promising to acknowledge Him in all my ways. I have not missed one day of this since asking the Lord for forgiveness of my sins. My journal and Bible have traveled to Key West,

Lilongwe, Johannesburg, Cape Town and the little-known village of Dowa in Central Africa. It has been to the Dominican Republic as I traveled with the Praying Pelican Mission with twelve of our youth from our church as my pastor continues to expose our young future church leaders to exciting ways to learn more about Jesus Christ. It has been to business trips, funerals, weddings, and family reunions. It keeps me humble, it keeps me fresh and hungry for more of what God has promised to all believers, and it gives me a head start out of the blocks each day to help thwart whatever silly ideas or notions that Satan throws my way.

I am also careful not to trade one addiction for another. I drink one cup of coffee a day, no lottery tickets for me, and I don't associate with men that have opposing points of view because 1 Corinthians 15: 33-34 reminds us, "Don't be misled. Bad company corrupts good character. Come back to your senses as you ought, and stop sinning for there are some who are ignorant of God--I say this to your shame." Life as an addict shows no gentleness or ease and all sins tend to be addictive, and the terminal point of addiction is damnation so if you are reading this book and your life is spinning out of control, remember to pray the Serenity Prayer: "God grant me the serenity to accept the things that I cannot change, the courage to change the things that I can, and the wisdom to know the difference."

I must have recited that prayer thousands of times just as a symbolic way to start a recovery meeting, but when I asked God to forgive me of my sins and reveal to me the way to eternal salvation, it was then, and not until then that my serenity was granted.

CPSIA information can be obtained
at www.ICGtesting.com
Printed in the USA
FSHW012132120519
58075FS